HUMAN INTELLIGENCE, COUNTERTERRORISM, & NATIONAL LEADERSHIP

HUMAN INTELLIGENCE,
COUNTERTERRORISM,
& NATIONAL LEADERSHIP

A PRACTICAL GUIDE

GARY BERNTSEN

Foreword by Seth G. Jones

Potomac Books, Inc.
Washington, D.C.

Published in the United States by Potomac Books, Inc. All rights
reserved. No part of this book may be reproduced in any manner whatsoever without written permission from the publisher,
except in the case of brief quotations embodied in critical articles and reviews.

All statements of fact, opinion, or analysis expressed herein
are the author's and do not reflect the official positions or views
of the CIA or any other U.S. government agency.

Nothing in the contents should be construed as asserting or
implying U.S. government authentication of information or
Agency endorsement of the author's views. This material has been
reviewed by the CIA to prevent the disclosure of classified information.

Library of Congress Cataloging-in-Publication Data
Berntsen, Gary.
 Human intelligence, counterterrorism, and national leadership:
a practical guide / Gary Berntsen ; foreword by Seth G. Jones. —
1st ed.
 p. cm.
 Includes bibliographical references and index.
 ISBN 978-1-59797-254-3 (alk. paper)
 1. Intelligence service—United States. 2. Terrorism—Prevention—Government policy—United States. 3. Counterinsurgency—United States. I. Title.
 JK468.I6B42 2008
 327.1273—dc22

                          2008021762

Printed in the United States of America on acid-free paper that
meets the American National Standards Institute Z39-48 Standard.

Potomac Books, Inc.
22841 Quicksilver Drive
Dulles, Virginia 20166

First Edition

10 9 8 7 6 5 4 3 2 1

Young American fighting men and women
and those of allied nations are sacrificing their lives and
bodies in a heroic struggle. Their sacrifice provides opportunity,
security, and hope for a better future to millions in the Middle
East and Southwest Asia. We have a responsibility to provide
leadership and sound decision-making worthy of their sacrifice.
God bless each and every one of them.

CONTENTS

FOREWORD

"O, where hath our intelligence been drunk?
Where hath it slept?"
—William Shakespeare, *King John*, Act 4, Scene 2

Shakespeare left us no play that was cast in an intelligence agency. He certainly had his reasons for missing such an opportunity. But had he seized it, he might well have given us another tragedy. U.S. policymakers would do well to heed Shakespeare's words today. The shape and nature of international relations have become increasingly fluid since the end of the Cold War and the September 2001 terrorist attacks in the United States, but American intelligence has not kept pace.

New security challenges confound the familiar frameworks that the intelligence community developed for collecting against, and then understanding, the capabilities and intentions of the Soviet Union and its allies. These threats have given way to a new set of adversaries with different objectives and capabilities. Intelligence must discern the behavior not just of states but also of nonstate actors, especially terrorists, who pursue new ways of fighting and do not adhere to familiar patterns. In these circumstances, evolutionary change in intelligence is not likely to suffice. If radical reshaping is required, then conceptual underpinnings for it will need to be reconsidered and developed.

American power has also created a paradoxical situation. The United States has an unprecedented quantitative and qualitative margin of superiority over other countries and groups. It enjoys decisive preponderance in all major underlying components of power: economic, military, and technological. However, this power asymmetry has increasingly caused adversaries to adopt innovative tactics and strategies, including, among others, the use of diffuse, linear organizational structures to fight the United States at home and abroad. The United States has increasingly faced multiple, often uncoordinated, linear groups, unlike the classical organizational structures modeled after Mao Tse-tung's vision of guerrilla war, which involve hierarchically structured organizations. Perhaps the clearest example is Iraq. A loosely knit conglomeration of secular Baathists and former regime elements, foreign jihadis, Sunni nationalists, and organized criminal groups intermittently gravitate toward one another to carry out armed attacks, exchange intelligence, trade weapons, and engage in joint training. Afghanistan is another example, where the United States faces an amalgam of organizations such as the Taliban, al Qaeda, the Haqqani Network, Hezb-i-Islami, and a range of tribal militia and criminal networks.

In this fluid environment, Gary Berntsen's *Human Intelligence, Counterterrorism, and National Leadership* comes at a critical juncture. It is eviscerating and provocative and pushes us to rethink core assumptions and practices. Readers may reject some of his conclusions and recommendations, but few will find them easy to disregard and all will find them critical to engage and grapple with. In the pages that follow, Berntsen challenges us at all levels. "The National Commission on Terrorist Attacks Upon the United States found institutional failures at all levels of government leading up to the attacks," he writes in his introduction. "What were beyond the scope of the commission's report were issues related to the identification of failures in leadership at the national level. Those failures belong to both major political parties in America."

Intelligence, especially human intelligence, is a core focus of the book. But it examines a panoply of issues, such as covert action, counterterrorism, counterinsurgency, interrogation, Iran, and weapons of mass destruction. These are some of America's most pressing challenges at home and abroad.

Berntsen is uniquely qualified to tackle these issues. He entered the Central Intelligence Agency (CIA) in 1982 and spent more than twenty-three years in the Clandestine Service, receiving the CIA's Distinguished Intelligence Medal and the Intelligence Star. His career included multiple assignments in the Middle East, South Asia, and Latin America, and he served as a CIA station chief on three separate occasions. He led several of the CIA's most important counterterrorism deployments, including its response to the East Africa bombings and the September 11, 2001, attacks. He is a true patriot, and his book is an important contribution to make America and the world safer.

Berntsen calls for fundamentally rethinking the CIA's personnel system. He argues that the most important element of the CIA's mission is its role as the nation's primary collector of human intelligence. Without a better personnel system to support operators who recruit and handle the CIA's clandestine sources, the culture of field service and risk-taking becomes exponentially diminished. The CIA's collection failures, Berntsen notes, are directly related to personnel decisions. Following the September 2001 attacks, it became cliché in the United States to talk about the CIA's "failure to connect the dots." In reality, Berntsen argues, the CIA's failure to *collect* the dots caused intelligence lapses. The consequences of placing unqualified personnel at the top of the Clandestine Service, the downsizing of the service, and the reengineering of a personnel system that did not adequately reward performance in operations all contributed to the CIA's inability to identify and disrupt the September 2001 attacks.

A related gap, he argues, is the lack of competent warriors who understand the culture, customs, and language of Islamic terrorists and jihadists. The British Empire, he points out, covered such diverse places as India, Pakistan, Nigeria, Hong Kong, Australia, and Fiji. One of the keys to Britain's success was a well-trained officer corps with significant linguistic capabilities. All of the officers in the British Indian Army, for example, were expected to give orders in the local language of their troops and were given handsome bonuses to be fluent in those languages. The U.S. military, Berntsen contends, must follow the British example. To face today's fluid international environment, he also recommends establishing a "Freedom Corps" comprising U.S. light infantry, combat engineers, and military police (roughly twenty thousand men and women) from the Islamic world. The majority of its enlisted soldiers, he notes, should be native Arabic, Farsi/ Dari, Pushtu, Uzbek, and Somali speakers. This corps would be trained and led by American soldiers primarily for counterinsurgency and counterterrorist missions.

Berntsen also addresses relations between the military and intelligence operators. In the course of ongoing conflicts, he writes, it is not only important to develop sources within insurgent and terrorist groups but to fully exploit such sources. Exploiting sources enables U.S. forces to identify and neutralize terrorist group leaders and members. What has worked best is fusing CIA or military operators on the ground with U.S. military strike capability, as during the overthrow of the Taliban regime in late 2001. Approximately 100 CIA officers, 350 Special Forces soldiers, and 15,000 Afghans—with the support of as many as 100 combat sorties per day—defeated a Taliban army estimated at 50,000 to 60,000 plus several thousand al Qaeda fighters. This was done in less than three months with only a dozen U.S. fatalities. The goal should be to permit immediate exploitation of intelligence in pursuit of emerging terrorist leaders and their key lieutenants. The CIA collects, documents, and disseminates its intelligence with speed. But when a manhunt against a key terrorist leader is under way, it is critical for military commanders to have immediate and continuing access to intelligence collection planning sessions. Embedding military officers in CIA field elements close to or on the battlefield provides a commander with the needed ability to keep up with the smaller, more nimble operational element and fully exploit opportunities that its presence and operations may create.

Berntsen tackles a range of other issues, such as the polygraph, arguing that it does more harm than good. At a time when the CIA is suffering a critical shortage of Middle Eastern linguists, he contends that the polygraph is the single largest deterrent to their employment. His recommendation is to limit its use to those who volunteer to serve in the CIA's Counterintelligence Center.

Human Intelligence, Counterterrorism, and National Leadership is designed to help policymakers better understand and prepare themselves for inevitable crises. And it does this well. It offers fresh, outside-the-box thinking and recommendations for some of America's most difficult challenges. As the Italian diplomat and political philosopher Niccolò Machiavelli wrote in *The Prince*, "Nothing is more dangerous or difficult than introducing a new order of things." Yet nothing is more important in a time of crisis. It is against this backdrop that Berntsen's book is both insightful and practical. "We are in a defining global struggle," he concludes. "The central question for America, as the preeminent political, economic, and military force on the planet, is, Do we have the will to fight and win? If so, are we prepared to organize ourselves in a fashion that will allow us to prevail?" The pages that follow provide important answers to these questions.

Seth G. Jones, Ph.D., is a political scientist at the RAND Corporation and adjunct professor in the Security Studies Program at Georgetown University. He is the author of In the Graveyard of Empires: America's War in Afghanistan *(Norton) and* The Rise of European Security Cooperation *(Cambridge University Press).*

PREFACE

I have had the privilege of serving my country abroad in the Middle East, South Asia, Europe, and Latin America for many years. I have seen significant political violence, insurgencies, and terrorism. I have witnessed governments attempt again and again to negotiate with killers who used ethnicity, religion, and ideology to justify horrific acts. And I have come to realize that all who participate in such terrorism could have easily entered the open, international political process and competed in the arena of free ideas. Many have even been offered amnesty. Yet still they commit acts that destroy families struggling to make better lives for themselves.

The war on the United States by Islamic terrorists and jihadists began well before September 11, 2001, and it has evolved into the defining global struggle we presently face. The central question for America, as the preeminent political, economic, and military force on the planet, is, Do we have the will to fight and win? If so, are we prepared to organize ourselves in a fashion that will allow us to prevail?

In this book I examine the practicalities of human intelligence and counterterrorism operations so that policymakers can better understand and prepare themselves for any international crisis that may arise. Future presidents and their staffs must approach the task of governing with the understanding that they will face dangerous challenges and horrific circumstances. What will matter on days when the terrible happens is not good intentions but preparation. It is my hope that this book will better prepare those in positions of responsibility to face the challenges ahead.

God Bless America.

May 2008

ACKNOWLEDGMENTS

During the course of my professional career in the CIA's Directorate of Operations, I had the good fortune of twice working for Fredd Snell, a very fine officer. Fredd was my boss, my mentor, and my friend. He invested an enormous amount of time and energy teaching me the craft. I in turn led and mentored others with Fredd's model, and we thus saved many lives. It was an incredible ride. Fredd is a man of high integrity with a passion for America. I would not have accomplished as much in my career had it not been for him. I dedicate this book to Fredd Snell.

I would like to thank Tim Tyler, Professor Neil Rossendorf of Long Island University at C. W. Post, and Professor Seth Jones of the RAND Corporation for their comments and recommendations on early drafts of the book. I would like to thank Capt. Blues Buckholz of the Oregon National Guard for his invaluable assistance. Blues's formal education and background in management and organizational leadership combined with his work on the ground with indigenous forces as a combat engineer in Helmand Province, among other areas in Afghanistan, made him an important contributor. I would like to thank Barbra Nixon, my sister, for her tireless efforts with multiple drafts and for finding a publisher for my policy book.

Finally, I would like to thank my wife, Estela, for her encouragement and support, and my daughter, Alexis, and son, Garrett, for their service to the country. No father is more proud of his children.

INTRODUCTION

At the opening of the twenty-first century, we have found advances in medicine, technology, and communications and an expansion of political freedom that do not necessarily translate into a more peaceful and stable world. Continued global population growth, accelerating urbanization, awakened subnational groups, and the global conflict between the West and Islamic jihadists and state sponsors of terrorism make for significant complexity and danger. I have drafted this book to serve as a guide to assist incoming presidents and White House staffs so that they may master the subject of human intelligence and counterterrorism operations in order to deal with this twenty-first century world. It is my hope that, after reading this, the next president and his or her staff will be able to draft a first directive, to be disseminated among the leadership of the intelligence and national security communities, outlining how the executive believes those communities should proceed to defend the nation's interests more adequately.

Having served for more than two decades in the Central Intelligence Agency's Clandestine Service in postings around the world, I have had unique opportunities to practice and lead human intelligence and counterterrorism operations. I hope to pass on understanding and insight that will aid policymakers in functioning at the highest level possible when dealing with these subjects.

The president nominates the director of national intelligence (DNI), the director of the Central Intelligence Agency (DCIA), and their respective deputies. The president and his or her cabinet members and White House staff are the primary consumers of intelligence as they make policy. It is the president's personal responsibility to ensure that the intelligence community is properly focused and functions in a manner that serves the national interest. Understanding intelligence and human intelligence operations is now equal in importance to understanding defense policy. Every president will have to work with a DNI and DCIA. The leadership and mastery of the appropriate subject material of all three of these officials will ultimately define whether these organizations succeed or fail. Failure to achieve mastery over this subject material will result in negative consequences for the people of the United States.

The twenty-first century began not on January 1, 2001, but on September 11, 2001, with al Qaeda's attacks on New York City, the Pentagon, and an aircraft that crashed in a field in Pennsylvania. The National Commission on Terrorist Attacks Upon the United States found institutional failures at all levels of government leading up to the attacks. The commission's review of the failures within the intelligence and national security communities and subsequent recommendations began long overdue reform and reorganization of those communities. What were beyond the scope of the commission's report, however, were issues related to the identification of failures in leadership at the national level. Those failures belong to both major political parties in America.

I will attempt to demystify the Clandestine Service and present a workable understanding of its function so that problems can be identified and prescriptions for improvement can be implemented. I will also examine intelligence and counterterrorism issues relevant to other parts of the national security community and provide recommendations in those fields of responsibility as well. We currently live in a time when small groups of individuals can leverage technology to conduct catastrophic attacks on our homeland, on our forces abroad, and against our allies. Such attacks and the reprisals launched by the United States and its allies bring challenges and consequences. The Clandestine Service and elements of the national security apparatus that work in unison provide the early warning needed to defeat attacks before they occur and defend what is most dear to us. It is my hope that this book will help us find a way forward in the struggle that lies ahead.

1. A LITTLE BACKGROUND

In the conduct of foreign policy and in the defense of the United States, the president of the United States and his or her key advisers, including the secretary of state, the secretary of defense, and the national security adviser, draw on multiple sources of information to make policy. A large portion of that information comes from overt sources such as books, newspapers, radio, television, and the Internet. Additionally, U.S. embassies operating in capital cities around the world provide a steady stream of reporting to policymakers in Washington, detailing the state of our relations with foreign governments, whether we maintain diplomatic relations with them or not.

Our embassies, which are also referred to as diplomatic missions, are led by an ambassador who is nominated by the president and confirmed by the U.S. Senate. The ambassador may be a career official of the Department of State—that is, a foreign service officer—or may be from outside the Foreign Service. Those from outside the Foreign Service are known as political appointees. Regardless of their backgrounds, ambassadorial nominees must sit before the Senate for confirmation and receive a majority vote. Ambassadorial nominees appointed when the Senate is out of session are called recess appointments and are required to face confirmation before the end of the Senate's next session.

Ambassadors and the foreign service officers under their command are responsible for the United States's daily interaction with host governments on a range of topics, including the maintenance of economic relations, military agreements, trade, cultural exchanges, and joint involvement in international organizations such as the United Nations. As mentioned previously, among an embassy's routine tasks is providing a steady stream of written reports and assessments detailing the state of relations between the United States and the local government.

1

Foreign governments around the world, whether friend or foe, share their intended policies and intentions with the United States to varying degrees. Most nations that the United States categorizes as allies or friends have a broad and deep relationship with the United States and seek to find ways to further mutual interests. Nations that are either openly or secretly hostile will not share their capabilities and intentions in the course of diplomatic relations. It is the principal responsibility of the Central Intelligence Agency (CIA) and other organizations within the intelligence community to collect information that hostile or competitor nations possess regarding their capabilities and intentions that will advance the ability of the U.S. president and his or her key advisers in making and implementing policy. How information is collected by the CIA and how it conducts other activities, such as covert action, in support of policy underlie the true state of our nation's intelligence capabilities. Only with an accurate understanding of what intelligence capabilities we possess can we begin to improve capabilities and fend off the increasing threats that exist in a world of growing danger.

CLANDESTINE INTELLIGENCE COLLECTION

In 2004 the cabinet-level position of director of national intelligence (DNI) was created with the passage of the Intelligence Reform and Terrorism Prevention Act. The DNI replaced the director of central intelligence (DCI) as the head of the sixteen organizations that make up the U.S. intelligence community. The DNI also assumed the role of principal intelligence adviser to the president and National Security Council (NSC). The DCI now focuses solely on his or her principal organization, the CIA, and a new title, the director of the Central Intelligence Agency (DCIA), reflects that change.

The CIA is made up of four basic components, which at times have been shuffled around and renamed but have essentially remained intact during the agency's five plus decades of existence: the Clandestine Service, which fulfills the CIA's primary mission—collection of intelligence through human sources—and has been known for most of the CIA's existence as the Directorate of Operations; the Directorate of Intelligence, which conducts analysis and writes finished intelligence for policymakers; the Directorate of

Science and Technology, which primarily handles major technical collection systems; and finally the Directorate of Administration, which manages the agency's resources and personnel. The Clandestine Service's mission, personnel, and leadership are the central focus of this book.

In 2005, to achieve better unity of effort in the field of human intelligence, the CIA's Directorate of Operations and the Department of Defense's Defense Humint Service (DHS) were merged to create a single organization called the National Clandestine Service (NCS). This combined service is directed by the chief of the NCS, who answers to the director of the CIA (DCIA) and the deputy director of the CIA (DDCIA) and is responsible for the broad spectrum of human intelligence operations conducted by the entire U.S. government. A cadre of operations officers (or case officers), collection management officers, and staff officers make up the Clandestine Service.

Operations officers are trained in the art of collecting human intelligence (HUMINT) and are deployed to elements around the globe referred to as stations, bases, and teams, depending on their size, location, and mission. A chief of station (COS) is a senior officer who leads the CIA's efforts in a country. The COS is also the DCIA's personal representative and serves as the principal intelligence adviser to the U.S. ambassador in the country. The COS manages operations officers in the acquisition and handling of human sources, including officials within hostile governments and terrorist organizations, weapons proliferators, and narco-traffickers threatening U.S. interests. These sources provide intelligence to the United States under the risk of identification, arrest, or death, and it is the COS's responsibility not to lose these sources. In those places where the CIA has an existing bilateral relationship with a host government's intelligence service, the COS will manage that relationship with the foreign intelligence service. The CIA station and allied foreign intelligence organizations frequently cooperate in operations against terrorist organizations and hostile governments. These are called *bilateral*, or *liaison*, *operations*.

The craft of acquiring and handling human sources is known as *espionage*. Espionage falls under the CIA's foreign intelligence (FI) mission and is the staple of the CIA's efforts abroad. Though other organizations in the United States, such as the Federal Bureau of

Investigations (FBI) and the Drug Enforcement Agency (DEA), handle clandestine sources for the purpose of conducting arrests concerning violations of U.S. law, only the CIA has the unique responsibility of human intelligence collection in support of policy.

Additionally, the CIA, at the direction of the president, conducts covert action. Covert action is any action employed by a government or entity to achieve some political or military result in which the initiating party conceals its involvement, support, or initiation of the act. Covert action is undertaken only when a document called a Presidential Finding, which explains the parameters of the assigned activity, is drafted and signed by the president. When the president signs such a document, the CIA then briefs the two congressional intelligence oversight committees—the Senate Select Committee on Intelligence (SCCI) and the House Permanent Select Committee on Intelligence (HPSCI)—on the contents of the finding. (Covert action is covered in more detail in chapter 2.)

THE FOREIGN SERVICE

During the course of my career, I was assigned as a chief of station on three separate occasions. It was my distinct honor to serve under a number of truly gifted U.S. ambassadors and their deputy chiefs of mission (DCMs). Politicians and the media have unfairly stereotyped members of our Foreign Service as uncaring, self-serving bureaucrats, but in my conduct of human intelligence and counterterrorist operations, I found my Foreign Service colleagues to be dedicated, brave, and willing to share both the physical and bureaucratic risks that accompany service and operations in the most dangerous parts of the world. I consistently found that American ambassadors and their DCMs were more willing to incur higher levels of risk in the support of an intelligence or counterterrorist operation in the field than was CIA headquarters. Personnel from the CIA and the Foreign Service serving together abroad feel the heat of threats equally, and in my experience, they were almost always in agreement regarding the need for dynamic responses to imminent threats.

Many critics of the U.S. Foreign Service do not understand the complexity of and competition among the economic and political interests that affect so many of the U.S. government's foreign affairs decisions. Press stories of several minutes almost never illustrate the full measure of complexity behind international problems. The U.S. Foreign Service/Diplomatic Corps is not an Ivy League elitist institution. It is an institution whose members come from every race, religion, and creed in America. Its members, like the CIA's officers, hail from every urban, suburban, and rural part of the United States. Our diplomats and the members of the Clandestine Service are America's sons and daughters and frequently don steel helmets and Kevlar vests in the conduct of our nation's service. Sadly, increasing numbers of them die in service.

CRITICAL APPOINTMENTS

On entry into office, U.S. presidents must select White House staff members, including a chief of staff and a national security adviser. Members of the White House staff and members of the National Security Council do not require Senate confirmation. However, cabinet members such as the secretary of state and the secretary of defense, the DNI, and the deputy director and director of the CIA all require both presidential nomination and confirmation with a majority vote from the Senate.

During the CIA's early years, a number of career intelligence officers, including Allen Dulles, Richard Helms, and William Colby, ascended to DCIA. Following the Watergate scandal in 1973, the U.S. Congress sought to expand its authority over what it viewed as excessive presidential power. The U.S. Senate Select Committee to Study Governmental Operations with Respect to Intelligence Activities (known as the Church committee for its chairman, Senator Frank Church of Idaho) and the House Select Committee on Intelligence (known as the Pike committee for its chair, Representative Otis Pike of New York) investigated and revealed numerous activities by the CIA, which they claimed violated the spirit and letter of U.S. law. These hearings took place in 1975 and 1976 and resulted in formalized congressional oversight of the CIA. After the Church and Pike reviews, the president began to look outside the CIA for directors who had a greater sensitivity to the agency's responsibilities to American society in a broader sense. Over the years, politicians, judges, ambassadors, businessmen, military officers, professors, Congress members, and congressional staff have been nominated and confirmed to hold the CIA's most senior positions.

While there is rarely a perfect candidate for CIA leadership, a president's first rule of thumb when choosing a DCIA should be to choose someone who will do no harm to the Clandestine Service. During the past thirty years two presidents have nominated and won confirmation for CIA directors who entered the office with the aim of reducing the Clandestine Service in personnel and capability: Admiral Stansfield Turner, who was nominated by Jimmy Carter, and John Deutch, who was nominated by Bill Clinton. During Turner's time at the CIA, the Soviet Union, with Cuba's help, reached its high-water mark in establishing leftist governments under force of arms in countries including Angola, Ethiopia, Mozambique, and Nicaragua, and it initiated civil wars in a half dozen other countries. Numerous historical factors contributed to communism's advancement internationally during this period, and it clearly was not an appropriate time to conduct a drawdown in clandestine collection. Similarly, in the mid-1990s John Deutch assaulted the Clandestine Service at a time when Islamic fundamentalism was constructing a worldwide movement to make war on America; Deutch's efforts can be viewed only as an act of unilateral disarmament.

Republican presidents often fare little better in ensuring the health of the Clandestine Service. President Reagan's choice for DCIA, William Casey, began his tenure by selecting businessman Max Hugel to run the CIA's then–Directorate of Operations. Though Mr. Hugel had held a junior position in the Office of Strategic Service (OSS) forty years before his appointment, he had little in terms of relevant experience in intelligence, foreign policy, or government that qualified him for the position. One would have thought that Casey, himself a former OSS officer, would have known better. Within a year the businessman was fired, and Casey was treated to a tongue-lashing from Senator Barry Goldwater regarding his severe lack of judgment in this matter.

The George W. Bush administration's handling of intelligence about Iraqi weapons of mass destruction damaged both the agency's and the White House's credibility. While Saddam Hussein, who was responsible for the death of more than a million people, was intolerable as the leader of Iraq, the misuse of intelligence as a pretext for war in this case was heartbreaking. The White House's decisions regarding Iraq set off a deadly chain of events. The administration's failure to put a sufficient number of forces on the ground to maintain order and its unwillingness to recognize the existence of a growing insurgency, even as CIA officers in the field pointed it out, contributed to the explosion in violence, terrorism, and sectarianism that we currently face in Iraq. (In an effort to reverse the taint on his administration brought by the September 11 attacks and the Iraq debacle, George W. Bush in 2006 selected Gen. Michael Hayden as DCIA and Steven Kappes as DDCIA. Both men are highly respected within the agency, understand all aspects of intelligence, and are strong leaders.)

In terms of bright spots, President George H. W. Bush made the collapse of Eastern Europe and fall of the Soviet Union seem a routine diplomatic task. Bush, a former DCIA, congressman, ambassador, and two-term vice president, brought a level of knowledge, skill, and character to the presidency that is unmatched in modern times. The fact that George H. W. Bush began his career in government at age eighteen as one of the youngest fighter pilots in World War II made him a hero across the CIA. As president, Bush chose the very capable Robert Gates, a career CIA analyst, as DCIA, Brent Scowcroft as his national security adviser, and James Baker as his secretary of state. Together the four used intelligence in a way that provided for informed and adroit policy during the most dangerous of times.

President Clinton's first DCI, James Woolsey, was capable and respected, and he understood the CIA. Unfortunately, he did not appear to have the confidence of the president. Woolsey resigned after only two years.

The selection of a talented and dedicated DNI and DCIA should be a goal of both political parties and the American people. At a minimum, candidates for these positions must possess relevant experience in foreign policy and in running a large bureaucracy, and most important, a demonstrated record of sound leadership in making life and death decisions. Senior military officers and ambassadors come with these experiences. The people of the United States cannot afford to wait a year or two for an appointee to get up to speed.

CHIEF OF THE NCS

Though the DNI and DCIA are important in intelligence collection, the chief of the National Clandestine Service, historically referred to as the Deputy Director of Operations (an officer at the assistant secretary level), is most important because he or she runs the CIA's Clandestine Service. The chief of NCS is tasked with leading the CIA's cadre of case officers, assigned at headquarters or globally, that conducts intelligence operations. Though it is not law, it is imperative this individual be a career member of the Clandestine Service who is recognized at the time of appointment as its most skilled and capable leader. As noted earlier in this chapter, William Casey named a businessman with little relevant experience to the position. During the Clinton administration, John Deutch named an officer who had spent almost his entire career as an analyst and possessed no foreign operational experience to lead the Clandestine Service. George Tenet selected an individual who had served only five years abroad. Most operations officers spend three times that amount conducting operations abroad. Even though all of these men were intelligent and cared deeply about the United States, none had either the hands-on operational experience needed or the full respect of the men and women they led. None took sufficient action to position the Clandestine Service, in terms of personnel, resources, and rules of engagement, to confront the growing threat of Islamic jihadists prior to 2001.

Presidents must take it on themselves to be involved in overseeing this critical selection by the DCIA. They must realize that the next chief of NCS does not have to come from existing senior officers but alternatively can be pulled from previously retired CIA officers. Future presidents should consult senior members of the Department of State, FBI, and CIA, as well as recently retired senior officers from each service. They should ask to personally review the service history of at least the five top candidates for the position. They must keep in mind that officers who have served as chiefs of station in hotspots and during conflicts have had a greater opportunity to exercise their command responsibilities than those who have been chiefs in safer locales. It is critical to view a respective candidate's service in contrast to the critical issues of the day. Where was an officer during the 1991 invasion of Kuwait or during the fall of the Soviet Union? What was an officer doing during the 2001 conflict in Afghanistan and the Iraq War? Officers who reached the Senior Intelligence Service while successfully avoiding the major conflicts of the past two decades—and many did just that—are not suited to lead the Clandestine Service. A president's failure to involve him or herself in the selection of a chief of the Clandestine Service can only be described as dereliction of duty.

PRESIDENT'S DAILY BRIEF

On a daily basis, the president and key policy advisers receive a document called the *President's Daily Brief* (PDB). Historically, analysts from the CIA's Directorate of Intelligence have prepared and delivered the PDB to the president and stood by to answer any follow-up questions he might ask. George Tenet, as the DCIA under George W. Bush, was the first director to accompany his analysts when they delivered the PDB. Porter Goss, who succeeded Tenet as DCIA, did the same. The first director of national intelligence, John Negroponte, continued the practice. PDB delivery does not require the presence of a cabinet-level officer, i.e., the DNI or the DCIA. The analysts who customarily delivered the brief were senior to mid-level officers who were extremely skilled, had PhDs, and had many years in the intelligence business. A president would be wise to simply schedule a weekly rather than daily meeting with the DNI or DCIA, both of whom should be present at their organizations, leading and managing their people, to the greatest extent possible. The intelligence community will not improve its collection if members of its leadership are more concerned with having daily face time with the president than with running their respective organizations.

CRITICAL POINTS

- Ninety-five percent of what is needed for policy is provided in open source reporting or by U.S. diplomatic missions abroad. The CIA's provision of intelligence provides only the final pieces necessary for the formulation of policy.

- The decisions of senior personnel, such as the DCIA and DDCIA, matter and echo throughout the system.

- Future presidents must involve themselves in the process of selecting the chief of the National Clandestine Service. The candidate must be a career officer recognized for success and leadership as a field officer, not a creature of CIA headquarters bureaucracy.

- The DNI or DCIA should not deliver the PDB on a daily basis; a weekly briefing is sufficient.

2. COVERT ACTION

The press and Hollywood like to portray covert action as the sexy staple of CIA activities. In reality, covert action has traditionally taken a backseat to the CIA's FI mission, i.e., recruiting and running sources to gain intelligence in support of policy. Covert action is defined as any action employed by a government or entity to achieve some political or military result in which the initiating party conceals its involvement, support, or initiation of the act. The CIA is the only organization in the U.S. government, with the exception of the Department of Defense during combat operations, permitted to conduct covert action. Most covert action operations have never been discussed publicly, and a number of them have advanced U.S. interests significantly.

Covert action may be lethal, as in war, or nonlethal. Nonlethal covert action could involve an intelligence service placing an article identifying a narcotics-trafficking organization as a threat to the public in a foreign newspaper. The article's aim would be to inform the population that the group was, for example, murdering individuals outside the organization. In such a press placement, the information must be truthful, factual, and substantiated. The press placement is termed "clandestine" because a government initiated or supported it in order to achieve some effect but did not reveal its role in the placement.

An example of covert action with lethal consequences is the CIA's involvement in the removal of Chilean president Salvador Allende during the early 1970s. When President Allende nationalized Chile's copper-mining industry against U.S. business interests, President Richard Nixon directed the CIA to secretly bring down the Allende government. The CIA used covert action to accomplish this task. It worked secretly with the Chilean press, labor unions, and contacts within the Chilean military establishment to destabilize President

11

Allende and eventually cause his overthrow. Thus covert action takes myriad forms and has numerous, sometimes unpredictable, results.

U.S. aid to the Contras in Nicaragua in the 1980s was a covert program that ultimately contributed to the restoration of democracy in Nicaragua. The CIA's covert support of the Afghan mujahideen in their fight against the Soviets in the 1980s resulted in the expulsion of the Soviets from Afghanistan and simultaneously set the stage for the emergence of Sunni extremism, which evolved into al Qaeda.

Covert action can be initiated in a number of ways. The president and his or her senior staff might recognize a significant problem exists that they believe cannot be dealt with successfully within normal diplomatic channels, with developmental projects, or with the overt deployment of military forces. In such a case, the president may order that a covert response be explored and drafted for his or her consideration. Alternatively, the CIA, Defense Department, or State Department may recognize that a particular problem can best be solved with covert action. In this case, the agency or department lobbies the policy community for its approval and implementation of the recommendation. Discussion of an agency's or department's recommendation for covert action most often takes place in the National Security Council or at the Deputies Committee, a committee of the deputies to senior cabinet officials. Once a consensus is reached within the policy community, a presidential finding is drafted and sent to the president for signature. Only after the president signs the finding are CIA personnel permitted to conduct the activities designated in the finding. The CIA then is obligated under law to conduct a notification, or official briefing on the nature of the covert action, of the two congressional intelligence oversight committees: the Senate Select Committee for Intelligence (SSCI) and the House Permanent Subcommittee on Intelligence (HPSCI).

COVERT ACTION TODAY

The attacks of September 11, 2001, clearly demonstrated the folly of a less than fully robust covert action program against Islamic jihadists overseas. Since the attacks, new covert action programs have been put in place, and the United States has made significant advances against the international jihadist movement that had openly declared war on it years earlier.

The aforementioned procedure for implementing covert action seems relatively straightforward: identify a need, place a request, sign a finding, notify Congress, and ultimately conduct the action. Unfortunately, this procession of events to conclusion is rare. Lawyers, interorganizational squabbles, and various policymakers' views are all at play here.

In its early years, the CIA's Clandestine Service was viewed as the Swiss army knife of the U.S. national security apparatus, and it was used in an array of covert action efforts all over the world. In recent years, as the CIA's bureaucracy has matured and as the National Security Council and the Departments of State, Defense, Treasury, and Justice have become participants in the discussion, it has become routine for requests coming up from the field to be killed early on. Competing interests and simple risk aversion destroy even the best-conceived covert action proposals before the president is given an opportunity to consider them. Only those covert action proposals initiated at the National Security Council have much of a chance of gaining acceptance. In truth, a major political fundraiser is in a better position than a CIA station chief to recommend covert action to the president.

Senior CIA operations officers in the field in particular find it difficult to obtain authority to use covert action to deal with emerging threats. Frequently, senior CIA officers running the Clandestine Service's headquarters bureaucracy will do everything in their power to defer, block, and argue against the employment of covert action. Covert action entails risk, and certain senior officers simply prefer to provide only intelligence to policymakers to avoid this risk. Taking on covert action also entails a responsibility for outcome, and few in the CIA's bureaucracy want such responsibility. Thus, the CIA's bureaucratic propensity is to block covert action requests at the lowest level possible. Even when a U.S. ambassador and chief of station are shoulder to shoulder in support of using covert action to counter a serious threat to U.S. interests, CIA Clandestine Service regional chiefs will order chiefs of station to stand silent. Bureaucratic cowardice has been endemic during significant periods of both Bill Clinton's and George W. Bush's administrations.

Of course, because President George W. Bush has launched

forces in both Afghanistan and Iraq, one might assume that he would not hesitate to use covert action. The problem for the current Bush administration is that Iraq has sucked the oxygen out of the air for foreign policy makers. Senior staff will not put any foreign policy action in front of the president unless it is relevant to Iraq, and the enormity of violence in Iraq has diminished the United States's ability to project itself into other parts of the world. Yet, there are presently hotspots in the world where minimal application of covert action could have a powerful and productive outcome.

The instructive point here is that ambassadors and chiefs of station who are closest to the action and first to recognize the need for covert action are rarely able to penetrate the political, administrative, and bureaucratic barriers established in Washington. The tendency in Washington is to stand back, wait, and hope for difficult situations to fix themselves. Individuals in Washington are never taken to task for inaction, and when a crisis arises because they took no action, they simply claim that the local political players acted irrationally, causing events to flare out of control. Doing nothing is always the safest course of action for individuals working to advance their careers in a bureaucracy, but it is not always in the best interests of the United States.

COVERT ACTION IN DEFENSE OF DEMOCRACY

Covert action was employed in the defense of democracy during the Cold War, but since the Soviet Union collapsed, it has been avoided except in cases of terrorism and narco-trafficking. During the Cold War, much of the CIA's covert action was aimed at defending the international community and fledgling democracies from the predatory practices of the Soviet Union and its proxy states. In these first years of the twenty-first century a myriad of threats to democracy and participatory governments have emerged around the world from a marriage of revolutionary and criminal elements. In Latin America a number of men under Cuban tutelage are willing to use whatever violence necessary to subvert democracy. Some of them, like Hugo Chávez, first tried to gain power with force. Failing with that approach, they have changed tactics, entering the democratic system itself to continue in their use of violence, intimidation, and murder. After decades of military rule, Latin American countries have established immunity for parliamentarians as a way to protect against the reestablishment of military dictatorships. The laws of immunity have provided the perfect platform from which this new breed of demagogue can launch a campaign of violence and intimidation to seize control of a nation.

Former Cuban president Fidel Castro's security apparatus provided the organizational skills and expertise for these takeovers. Venezuelan president Hugo Chávez, Castro's protégé, is providing the funding and populist rhetoric that has enabled Evo Morales to assume the Bolivian presidency and indigenous leader Ollanta Humala to make it to the final round of presidential balloting in Peru in 2005. Leftist candidate Andrés Manuel López Obrador came within a hair of taking power in Mexico in 2006. Ecuador's president Raphael Correa announced just after the recent death of a senior FARC official that he will no longer support U.S. regional counternarcotic efforts. The current Bush administration has stood slack jawed as political events in Latin America have taken a serious turn for the worse. CIA officers in the field there have repeatedly asked Washington to provide them the authority to confront the assault on democratic governments, but their requests have gone unheeded. The shift to the left in Latin America is not, as some would have us believe, a natural phenomena. It has been engineered by the combined and focused efforts of Castro's security services with Venezuelan financial support.

The CIA should absolutely be allowed to practice covert action to defend fledgling democracies. It is wishful thinking to believe that individuals with backgrounds in narco-trafficking, military coups, and murder will moderate or reform themselves once they enter the political process or are sworn into office. Still, the U.S. executive bureaucracy prefers to accept political defeat through inaction over incurring the risks associated with working actively to block undemocratic takeovers.

Because of the nature of covert action and the sensitivity of the related tradecraft and mechanisms, a full and open discussion of the subject is not possible. A new administration needs to quickly come to terms with what the Clandestine Service can and cannot do when it comes to covert action so that it is aware of all its potential options when dealing with foreign nations. Though covert action for counterterrorism and counternarcotics has become standard and accepted by policymakers and implementers, a major effort needs to be made to define what acceptable nonlethal covert action can be codified and standardized regarding defense of democracies.

Once new covert action tools are devised, they should be placed in the hands of CIA station chiefs, who, under a U.S. ambassador's authority, will determine the tools' initial use. This will trigger both the Department of State and CIA headquarters to review the actions and decide either to continue them or to cease activities. The use of limited preapproved nonlethal covert action in the field will compel policy discussion via its implementation and the subsequent congressional notification. This would effect a timely discussion and a level of accountability in Washington that does not currently exist.

I do not advocate the employment of covert action simply to intervene in the internal affairs of other nations. I advocate its employment to help defend democratic institutions that have required much sacrifice and effort to construct.

CRITICAL POINTS

- Covert action is any action taken secretly by representatives of a government in which the initiating government seeks to conceal its role in the action.

- The CIA is the principal organization in the U.S. government tasked with conducting covert action and can do so only with a signed presidential finding.

- The CIA is required to conduct a briefing (or notification) of the congressional oversight committees, SSCI and HPSCI, before it conducts covert action.

- Though using covert action to combat terrorism and narco-trafficking is accepted practice, it is extremely difficult to gain a presidential finding for covert action in the defense of democracy.

- Future presidents must understand the full range of options open to them in dealing with international challenges and must ensure that ambassadors and chiefs of station in the field present them with a full range of options for dealing with specific countries.

- CIA station chiefs, under U.S. ambassadors' approval, must be given the authority to defend democracy with limited nonlethal covert action tools that would then compel Washington bureaucrats to engage in the process of deciding whether to continue, expand, or cease such actions. Washington bureaucrats should not be permitted to remain uncommitted to action.

3. PERSONNEL: LIFEBLOOD OF THE CLANDESTINE SERVICE

From 2004 to 2006, CIA Director Porter Goss was reported to have stated on several occasions to various senior CIA managers, "I don't do personnel." He had relegated disputes between the senior managers and his personal staff to his highly partisan chief of staff. To the horror of the rank and file, Goss's inability to manage personnel compelled the CIA's deputy director of operations at the time, the widely respected Steve Kappes, to resign in November 2004. Goss failed to understand that DDO Kappes had risen through the ranks not because of politics or favoritism but through skill, commitment, sacrifice, and powerful leadership. The Clandestine Service had experienced years of weak leadership and, with Kappes at its head, was, in the view of many, on the verge of being restored. Before Kappes's resignation, most officers respected Director Goss because he had been a case officer in his early years and seemed to understand the necessity of risk in agency operations and to be attuned to the Clandestine Service's conservative ranks. The resignation, however, caused a massive loss of faith in Goss's judgment, especially when a steady stream of senior operations officers followed the DDO out the door.

Director Goss is a decent man who served his country honorably in the U.S. military, as an operations officer in the CIA, as a U.S. congressman, and finally as DCIA. Had he not considered himself above "doing personnel," the people of the United States would have been better served. DCIAs who want to be effective "do personnel."

HIRING AND TRAINING PERSONNEL

The Central Intelligence Agency hires individuals into its

Clandestine Service through a program called the Career Service Training (CST) program. With a minimum of a four-year college degree, one can apply to join the CIA as an operations officer or as another type of officer who supports operations. The CIA looks for career service trainees who are U.S. citizens, both male and female, who have a high level of intelligence, a demonstrated ability to learn foreign languages, a history of travel abroad, the ability to interact well with others, and a high level of personal motivation. Previous military experience is a plus. An applicant must undergo a security background check and a polygraph examination. Given the ongoing war with Islamic jihadists, speakers of Arabic, Persian, Urdu, and Pashto are in demand, as are those who speak Chinese and Russian.

If selected and cleared for the program, applicants are provided with extensive operational training in agent (human source) acquisition and handling. They learn how operations officers identify potential agents and then convince them to serve as sources of sensitive information about governments and groups hostile to the United States. They learn how an officer handles this relationship and collects intelligence without the source being compromised and captured. After this training, career trainees undergo language instruction and other types of specialized training that prepare them for specific assignments abroad. Training provides a basic understanding of the business; young officers truly learn the craft of espionage under the close supervision of senior officers during their first two tours in the field.

SHIFT IN FOCUS

From the early 1950s to the early 1990s, the agency's emphasis was on field service. Careers were advanced most rapidly when an officer took on multiple difficult field assignments one after the next and established a pattern of success. In the mid-1990s a major change to the CIA personnel system occurred. Under John Deutch and George Tenet, the agency ordered its officers to terminate relationships with assets (clandestine sources) with questionable pasts. Deutch and Tenet also reduced the size of the Clandestine Service and put in place significant levels of oversight from headquarters to ensure that mistakes did not occur. These DCIAs appeared to have little concern that opportunities for success would be reduced drastically with the implementation of greater bureaucracy. Those who agreed with the gutting of the Clandestine Service lined up for advancement. Those who understood the danger to national interest and resisted the reorganization were retired, fired, or relegated to jobs lacking consequence. Many officers who had never served in a position of field command ascended to senior positions in the Clandestine Service. Prior to Deutch's tenure, operations officers had held a large percentage of senior positions in the CIA's Senior Intelligence Service, but the 1990s was a time for headquarters staff officers, administrative officers, and other specialists who took little personal or career risk to seize a larger portion of the management pie. As a result, advancement opportunities for operations officers were reduced. Those ambitious for advancement left the operations track as quickly as possible and were rewarded for the move.

The single most important element of the CIA's mission is its role as the nation's primary collector of foreign human intelligence. Without a personnel system that supported the principal actors in the CIA, i.e, the operations officers, the culture of field service and risk taking was diminished. The CIA's collection failures, as outlined after the September 11 attacks, are directly related to these personnel decisions. Following September 11, 2001, it became cliché in the United States to talk about the CIA's failure to *connect* the dots. In reality, as former Associate Deputy Director for Operations Jack Devine so accurately explained in a *New York Times* op-ed, the CIA's failure to *collect* the dots caused the intelligence lapses. The combined failure to recognize the consequences of placing unqualified personnel at the top of the Clandestine Service, the downsizing of the service, and the reengineering of a personnel system that did not as its primary function reward performance in operations contributed to the CIA's inability to identify and disrupt the attacks on September 11.

CULTIVATING KNOWLEDGE WORKERS

In 1998 former Labor Secretary Robert Reich wrote a book called *Work of Nations*, in which he ably discussed the importance of knowledge workers. Reich points out that though building a factory may be costly and though equipping it with robots and computers may be complicated, personnel still remain the most important element in twenty-first-century factories. Individuals who have been educated for thirteen years at public expense, most of whom have an additional two, four, and six years of university education and the ability to work with technology, constitute the true value of a company. Reich goes on to expound on the principle of maintaining a base of knowledge workers and the huge investment required of a society to produce and maintain such a work force.

The Clandestine Service is the ultimate collection of knowledge workers in the United States. Operations officers with four years of college, important military and language skills, and certain personal characteristics and training know how to function in complex foreign societies and can penetrate even the most closed segments of hostile foreign groups to produce intelligence for U.S. policymakers.

The Clandestine Service's focus needs to be how it can create a personnel system tied to the acquisition of new sources and the production of critical intelligence in support of policymakers. Since the mid-1990s, the most ambitious officers in the Clandestine Service have sought minimal time in the field and burrowed themselves in CIA headquarters bureaucracy to attain advancement.

The next president, responsible for ensuring the nation's safety, needs to break this cycle. For the next four years, he or she should encourage the promotion of only operations officers with significant field experience in order to reestablish the culture of overseas service. In addition, he or she should prevent officers from taking successive jobs in headquarters in order to ensure greater employee development.

Future presidents also need to understand the Clandestine Service's size and relative capacity for action. If they fail to devote time to this, they will likely find themselves in a dilemma during upcoming conflicts, which may require additional intelligence resources that are unfortunately unavailable. The FBI has approximately thirty thousand employees. Roughly thirteen thousand are classified as special agents and are qualified to conduct investigations and fieldwork among the U.S. population of 300 million. The CIA has a force of operations officers that is but a small fraction of the thirteen thousand special agents. Operations officers must manage both headquarters operations and staff billets around the world, providing intelligence and countering threats on a planet of 6.5 billion people.

Shortly after he was confirmed as director, Porter Goss told President Bush that the Clandestine Service was woefully understaffed and did not have the capacity to deal with the threats that faced the nation. Bush was troubled when he learned of how small certain CIA stations were and surprised to hear the actual number of operations officers. He ordered that the Clandestine Service be doubled in size as quickly as possible. This order came four years after Bush's first inauguration. Though the act was welcome, it betrayed the fact that he had not sought an accurate understanding of the size and needs of the Clandestine Service during his first term in the White House. Presidents must tackle the issues central to the performance of U.S. intelligence capabilities on their first days in office, not during the early days of their second term.

CIA staff and officers are federal employees and are governed by federal personnel and retirement regulations. Given the importance and unique nature of intelligence collection and the difficulty involved in penetrating terrorist groups, it is critical that the president work with the Congress to establish a provision whereby a small cadre of highly skilled operations officers, possibly numbering only one hundred, with unique native language skills or high-end counterterrorism skills be allowed to conduct only field operations for the Clandestine Service over a period of ten or fifteen years, rather than the standard federal minimum of twenty years. A great number of U.S. citizens, because of age or other personal circumstances, cannot provide a lifetime of service to the CIA but possess skills that might literally save the nation. Future presidents must help the CIA by altering the personnel system to allow shorter-term hiring attached to high-end field service and intelligence collection.

CRITICAL POINTS

- The president must make it a priority to understand the size and capabilities of the Clandestine Service on taking office and address any problems immediately.

- The president must ensure that a personnel system is put in place that rewards those who do the Clandestine Service's most critical work: acquiring and handling sources.

- The president should work with Congress to attain approval to create a special career category of operations officers for those who have critical skills but fall outside the prescribed age limits for service. Creating a special prorated retirement system would make such a program attractive and strengthen collection.

4. THE POLYGRAPH:

EATING OUR YOUNG

The use of the polygraph, or lie detector, within the Central Intelligence Agency and the national security community receives little public attention but is critically important to address. The polygraph is used as a prescreening tool for employment at the CIA and is also part of the security reinvestigations process for current employees.

Mark Zaid, a noted national security attorney, testified extensively in front of Congress on the polygraph in April 2001.[*] The following paraphrases his description of the polygraph process: A polygraph exam, or modern lie detector test, measures respiration at two points on the body: the upper chest and the abdomen. Movements of the body associated with the rate and depth of breathing are recorded at these points. The polygraph also measures perspiration with attachments on the subject's fingertips. Finally, a blood pressure cup allows for cardiovascular measurements.

The polygraph examiner asks the subject routine questions that are known to be true and false in order to establish baseline measurements. Then the examiner uses the baseline measurements to judge the subject's responses to a series of questions pertaining to his or her lifestyle, potential drug use, sexual relations, and contact with foreign nationals. Individuals whose physical responses register outside the baseline are claimed to be either deceptive (lying) or inconclusive (unresolved).

---

[*] Prepared statement of Mark S. Zaid Esq., in Senate Committee on the Judiciary, *Issues Surrounding Use of Polygraph: Hearing before the Committee on the Judiciary*, 107th Cong., 1st sess., April 25, 2001.

The government itself acknowledges that the polygraph provides false positives as often as 15 percent of the time. That means 15 percent of those the test indicates are lying are not lying; their physiological reactions to questions is the result of something else, such as nervousness. This level of inaccuracy is the reason polygraph results are not admissible as evidence in a court of law.

I believe that polygraph programs administered by the U.S. government as part of routine prescreening and security reinvestigations do far greater harm than good. The problem is that those who manage the CIA's personnel system recognize that the exam is not 100 percent correct but base their personnel decisions on polygraph results as though they are accurate.

An individual whose polygraph exam results indicate deception will not be hired. To support the decision not to hire the individual, the CIA officer responsible for the applicant's background investigation will aggressively seek derogatory information in the person's past or the agency will simply deny the person employment based on psychological makeup. The CIA has established a system that allows its officers to testify in front of Congress that no applicant has ever been turned down or fired solely because of an unresolved polygraph. But this simply is not true. Many honest citizens with desperately needed skills, like Arabic and Persian language ability, are turned away, and loyal, hardworking officers are made to endure days of additional testing and interrogations and even investigation by the FBI. Further, subjects whose tests are determined to demonstrate deception or have inconclusive results have little recourse.

In the wake of the arrest and prosecution of CIA officers Aldrich Ames and James Nicholson and FBI special agent Robert Hanssen, all of whom actively provided sensitive information to the Russians causing terrible damage to U.S. intelligence, calls were made to do more to protect against hostile intelligence threats. Hanssen had never taken a polygraph, and Ames had apparently managed to pass his exam, yet the CIA and other national security organizations responded to each of the arrests by increasing the use of the polygraph to show that they were taking action.

During the course of my career I was given a polygraph exam four times. Each time I was tested, I was treated fairly and with respect, and my tests never took much more than an hour. Unfortunately, many of my colleagues suffered at the hands of the Office of Security's polygraph examiners, who hold an enormous amount of power. Their examiners used the polygraph exams to fish for threats and to make wild accusations of secret, treasonous cooperation with foreign intelligence services. Honest, loyal, and brave officers had their careers and lives destroyed in this process. In fact, several years ago hundreds of officers were placed in investigation limbo because of the polygraph, and the American Civil Liberty Union (ACLU) was brought in to relieve the CIA's work force from the insanity.

Mark Zaid also testified to Congress on the polygraph's historical use. He said that in the past twenty years there has been government research on the polygraph, and incredibly, most of what is in print recommends against its use. In November 1983 the Office of Technology Assessment issued a report entitled "Scientific Validity of Polygraph Testing," which concluded that "the available research evidence does not establish the scientific validity of the polygraph test for personnel security screening" and that the "mathematical chance of incorrect identification of innocent persons as deceptive (false positives) is highest when the polygraph is used for screening purposes." In response to this report and other research, the Employee Polygraph Protection Act of 1988 was enacted. It generally prohibits the private sector from using polygraphs in preemployment screening and sharply curtails permissible uses of the polygraph in specific incident investigations. Before this legislation was enacted, it was estimated that every year a minimum of 400,000 truthful employees were wrongfully labeled deceptive and suffered adverse employment consequences. Yet, the federal government, even in light of this finding, exempted itself from the provisions of prohibiting preemployment testing.

Former attorney general John Ashcroft announced his intention to expand the polygraph's use, despite the 15 percent false positive rate. Even with twenty years' of research backing the elimination of polygraph testing, innocent people continue to be falsely accused and no protection exists in any agency to address this problem. Mr. Zaid noted, "Most recently, the FY2000 Intelligence Authorization Act asserted that 'polygraphing has been described as "a useful, if unreliable," investigative tool.' The Senate Intelligence Committee instructed the Central Intelligence Agency and FBI to assess 'alternative technologies to the polygraph' and report back to the Committee within ninety days."

RECOMMENDATIONS

There is no doubt that the polygraph is a useful interrogation tool, and I do not oppose its occasional use on specific, narrow topics when an incident or event has occurred. But making employment decisions based solely on a polygraph result, without corroborating evidence, does more harm than good to an organization. The CIA's current policies regarding the polygraph are counterproductive, and an incoming president should curtail the polygraph's employment. A president must ask, Does the additional benefit the polygraph provides as a deterrent to internal criminal behavior or defense from foreign penetration outweigh the need to get the most highly skilled people into the service of defending the nation?

The polygraph's use as a prescreening tool should be limited to applicants who volunteer to serve in the CIA's Counterintelligence Center, the organization within the CIA that is tasked with defending the CIA and U.S. government from hostile penetration—that is, the place a hostile service would most want to penetrate. The best way to know if a hostile service is running sources within the CIA is not to interrogate every CIA officer in service but rather to penetrate hostile services running operations against us. The vast majority of America's most important counterintelligence successes came not from the FBI uncovering a traitor's actions with police work or interrogation but rather from the CIA's penetrations of hostile intelligence services. In the intelligence business a really good offense is the best defense.

One of the primary targets of CIA polygraph tests is applicants and employees who have substance abuse problems. A more practical way to determine whether someone has a drug problem is to institute mandatory random urinalysis and drug testing for all applicants and employees.

The CIA polygraph test also targets those who have significant contact with foreign nationals. I recommend setting up a tier system of security clearances to provide more employment opportunities for native Arabic, Persian, Pashto, and Urdu speakers. Those who cannot be issued top secret clearance because they interact frequently with family members who are foreign nationals, should be given only provisional secret clearances and opportunities to serve as translators or in less sensitive positions. As part of this process, I recommend creating independent counterterrorist operational elements made up of officers led by cleared senior operations officers. Those operations would be highly compartmentalized to reduce the loss of intelligence information should a unit be targeted successfully for enemy penetration.

The CIA still cannot adequately staff its billets with fully trained case officers possessing the needed language skills in the Middle East even though it has a population of five million Muslim Americans from which to hire. Cleary something is terribly wrong. The bureaucracy, in terms of security clearances, is broken and needs intervention. The manner in which security clearances are handled (i.e., via the polygraph) directly relates to our inability to field officers with sufficient language abilities.

CRITICAL POINTS

- The polygraph and its overall results have not been reported accurately to the president and Congress. The polygraph does more harm than good.

- At a time when the CIA is suffering a critical shortage of Middle Eastern linguists, the polygraph is the single largest deterrent to their employment and the accomplishment of securing the United States from the threat of violent attack.

- Maintaining the polygraph's use in the Counterintelligence Center is recommended because service in counterintelligence is voluntary and that section is most likely to be targeted by a foreign intelligence service.

5. COUNTERTERRORISM:

INTELLIGENCE, LAW ENFORCEMENT, AND MILITARY POWER

Foremost among any president's responsibilities is keeping the nation safe from terrorism. To accomplish this mission the president has many tools, including policy, diplomacy, trade, intelligence, law enforcement, and military power. In this chapter, I will focus on intelligence, law enforcement, and military power, examining first offensive operations outside the United States and then looking at defensive measures taken within U.S. borders. I will deal with counterterrorism policy in chapter 11.

THE PLAYERS

The CIA is the primary arm of the U.S. government to conduct counterterrorist operations abroad, and it fulfills this mission primarily via clandestine human source operations. These operations are conducted either by the U.S. officers alone or by U.S. officers in conjunction with foreign powers. The CIA has a capability for HUMINT that no other U.S. government agency possesses, as well as the legal mandate for intelligence collection operations.

The FBI, the premier U.S. law enforcement agency, has in the past few years increased the number of FBI offices abroad from forty-seven to more than seventy-five. The FBI officers designated as legal attachés also have a role in the counterterrorism mission. The CIA's greater commitment of resources, global coverage, and deep and long-standing relationships with host intelligence services makes the agency the senior partner in its relationship with the FBI in the foreign counterterrorism environment; the officer who possesses the source of intelligence on a particular threat determines the direction and handling of a case.

The CIA also works against terrorists threatening foreign countries and their interests. The CIA covers groups acting against foreign interests in order to either support democracy or to maintain regional stability. Unlike the CIA, the FBI does not have a responsibility to report on regional terrorist groups and instead focuses its resources solely against terrorist groups or persons planning attacks on U.S. citizens or interests.

The last significant U.S. government asset in counterterrorism missions abroad is the federal law enforcement officer called a regional security officer (RSO) assigned to every U.S. embassy around the globe. RSOs are Department of State Bureau of Diplomatic Security (DS) personnel who are primarily responsible for protecting the personnel and property of each U.S. embassy. They have local management responsibility for the Marine Corps Security Detachment, command the embassy's local guard force of up to six hundred security guards, and manage local investigators searching for missing Americans. RSOs are frequently the only U.S. law enforcement personnel on the ground and contribute significantly to the defense of American lives and property. Whereas historically only a few FBI agents have been fortunate enough to be selected for the FBI's attaché program and service abroad, all DS agents serve the majority of their careers in the foreign environment and develop impressive skill sets.

Finally, we cannot forget the numerous foreign sources the CIA's operations officers recruit abroad. Much has been made of the CIA's purported failure to recruit sources from within terrorist groups as opposed to those from within political and economic targets. It is rarely difficult to identify sources within hostile governments, as key decision-makers and targets for human source recruitment operations are relatively obvious. Access to individuals with political and economic information is thus easier to develop and maintain than is access to terrorists, who are not as easily identified. Unlike public figures, terrorists are not often invited to cocktail parties or diplomatic receptions. Further, it is difficult—though not impossible—to sustain contact with terrorists once they are identified. The violent nature of terrorists' lives and careers complicates the handling process and necessitates never-ending terrorist recruitment operations so that these highly perishable assets can be quickly replaced.

MANAGING TERRORIST EVENTS

A major terrorist attack against U.S. interests abroad, such as the attacks on the U.S. embassies in Nairobi, Kenya, and Dar es Salaam, Tanzania, in 1998 or the attack on the USS *Cole* in Yemen in 2000, is no longer treated as an intelligence operation but rather as a law enforcement case. Thus the FBI is responsible for the investigation following such an attack. The bureau chooses a senior officer to lead a deployment of several hundred officers along with significant legal, forensic, post-blast, investigative, and analytic muscle to the site of the attack. U.S. intelligence assets, including CIA teams or stations functioning on the ground, retain full authority over their intelligence operations but are required to focus those operations on supporting the FBI team.

As mentioned previously, the FBI has few opportunities for its almost thirteen thousand agents to serve in multiyear assignments abroad. Building more billets for the FBI outside the United States, especially in the Middle East, would be helpful in securing a large base of officers with greater knowledge and skill in understanding and fighting terrorists abroad, including Islamic jihadists. Given that Congress has limited the number of FBI offices abroad, it would be beneficial to assign twenty-five to fifty newly hired FBI agents each year to rotational positions in the Department of State's Bureau of Diplomatic Security. FBI agents serving on rotational assignments as junior RSOs would gain important foreign law enforcement experience and at the same time provide DS with additional manpower for the ever-growing challenges they face in the foreign environment.

THE U.S. MILITARY AND COUNTERTERRORISM

With the U.S. military's invasions of Afghanistan and Iraq, America has become both heavily engaged in the struggle against Islamic jihadists and the principal target of these same Islamic jihadists. In the decades prior to September 11, 2001, the U.S. military played only a limited role in U.S. efforts against Islamic extremists.

With the initial deployment of U.S. Army Special Forces teams attached to CIA elements for Operation Enduring Freedom in 2001, the United States fielded a lethal combination of airpower and a standing force of insurgents (the Northern Alliance). This combination toppled a Taliban and al Qaeda force much larger than itself. Neither the CIA nor the Special Forces would have enjoyed this level of success operating on its own. The military had few Special Forces officers and team members with relevant language or area experience, and the soldiers did not possess any recent experience in dealing with Afghan insurgent forces. The CIA had those abilities but lacked the military's logistics infrastructure and firepower.

The Iraq War (Operation Iraqi Freedom), in contrast, was planned and executed not as part of a counterterrorism campaign but rather as a conventional invasion. Though it is debatable whether Saddam Hussein was sufficiently contained and whether the invasion and accompanying violence has made the world a safer place, the U.S. military bears the brunt of attempting to bring order to an extremely difficult situation in Iraq on a daily basis. In Iraq sectarian killings, foreign terrorists, militias, Iranian interference, and horrific street violence have exceeded our worst fears. At the cost of four thousand dead and thirty thousand wounded, the U.S. military has been given the opportunity to develop improved urban counterinsurgency and combat counterterrorist tactics.

Within the Afghan and Iraq theaters of operation the U.S. military has expanded its intelligence collection and analysis to support its operations to build governments that are participatory and that respect citizens' individual rights. U.S. military commanders receive reports from the State Department, CIA, and NSA to supplement their own collection and reporting. This reporting is designed to give commanders the fullest possible understanding of the battlefield as they adjust tactics to meet an ever-evolving insurgent- and terrorist-filled environment.

A future president and his or her policymaking staff must ask the question, To what extent should the U.S. military be permitted to expand its intelligence operations in support of counterterrorism missions outside major battlefields? Some in the CIA would instinctively like to halt an expansion of any and all military intelligence operations outside those theaters. Given the expansion of jihadist networks globally and the CIA's personnel limitations, the military's participation in intelligence collection should be welcomed—but only after command, control, consultation, and training issues have been adequately addressed.

The president must write an executive order stating clearly that the U.S. ambassador, as the president's personal representative in country, should be briefed before combat commanders initiate intelligence operations in a country where that ambassador is assigned. The ambassador would need from the military only a general outline of the proposed initiative, not necessarily all of the specifics. Because ambassadors and their DCMs encounter intelligence and source protection issues on a daily basis, they can be relied on not to expose or impair any military operations. Thus, such an executive order will avert uncoordinated activities and political embarrassments.

The U.S. military has case officers, like those in the CIA, who train side by side with their CIA counterparts and perform to similar standards. But the U.S. military has not provided sufficient career opportunities, training, and advancement for military intelligence officers in general and military source handlers in particular.

Similarly, the military's attaché program is lacking in substance. All military attachés serve the dual role of representing the Department of Defense to host nations and overtly collecting intelligence for the Defense Intelligence Agency (DIA). Most military attachés begin their careers as armor officers, pilots, or submariners. They enter the attaché path late in their careers and learn their duties quickly. Creating further problems, the military, which historically refuses to promote attachés, discourages them from serving two consecutive tours and instead encourages them to return to their primary careers. If an attaché asks for a second tour in another embassy, he or she is risking career death and will most likely retire at his or her current grade. The irony is that attachés are always more productive on their second tour than they were on their first.

Successive directors of the Defense Intelligence Agency have talked about addressing this problem but have failed to act. The U.S. military would be wise to allow its attachés who are colonels to take successive assignments as they are promoted up to flag rank, i.e., to general or admiral. Attachés are the DIA's overseas eyes and ears, and they should be provided the fullest in career opportunities rather than be relegated to second-class status.

Another major problem facing the military is the large number of individuals serving in intelligence billets who are unprepared and undertrained for their duties. Young enlisted and noncommissioned officers serve on human collection teams (HCTs) that conduct source operations on battlefields. These young men and women bravely face the dangers of tactical intelligence field collection in Iraq and Afghanistan and yet are denied the tools to succeed. HCTs must receive area studies before deployment and be provided some language training. None of the HCT members I have met have had any such training.

Those managing the HCT system need to make it easier for their intelligence collectors to task new contacts and significantly increase the amount of funds at the HCTs' disposal so they are not tempted to pay sources out of their own pockets—a practice that is currently a huge problem. HCTs are on the front lines in the war on terrorism and are not served well by the DOD. Simply put, the Defense Department's HUMINT community needs to overhaul its doctrine, rewrite its regulations, and be allocated additional financial resources. To complete this overhaul, the DOD will need to bring in a senior CIA officer: no one currently in the DOD has the sufficient experience or the will to take and break the family china.

TYPES OF TERRORIST EVENTS ABROAD

Every terrorist event that occurs abroad involves different factors that will affect the U.S. government's levels of interest and involvement. If, for example, a cafe is bombed in the Middle East and all the victims are citizens of the host nation, not U.S. citizens, the United States has an intelligence interest in the technical and political aspects of the attack and its consequences but not a law enforcement interest. If victims of this hypothetical attack are U.S. citizens, the U.S. government will have both an intelligence and a law enforcement interest and, following U.S. law, will pursue and prosecute the attackers if they can be identified, captured, and transported to the United States.

Though U.S. law enforcement officers have no jurisdiction outside the United States, allied and friendly governments will frequently permit them to support local investigative efforts in an advisory role. The United States has extradition treaties with many of the world's nations that allow for the legal transfer of a prisoner in the custody of a foreign government to U.S. custody. In 1995, under an executive order issued by President Clinton, the practice of rendition was authorized for the CIA. The order allows a criminal or terrorist captured in one country by the U.S. or other forces to be moved, without the legal extradition process, to another country, where charges exist against the individual.

In an airline hijacking case, the nation that owns the aircraft has an interest, the nations each passenger holds citizenship in have an interest, and the country where the plane lands has an interest—and a huge responsibility to the international community. It must act in a way that will advance the interests of the passenger-victims without rewarding the terrorists. In 1988 Hezbollah hijacked Kuwait Airways Flight 422, which originated in Bangkok, and landed the aircraft temporarily in Iran. The Iranian government allowed additional terrorists and weapons on board the aircraft in support of the original hijackers. The terrorists eventually murdered Kuwaiti citizens who were on the aircraft.

Few countries in the world have the resources, organization, or people qualified to successfully resolve a hijacking or barricade situation without a huge loss of life or costly concessions. It is critical that any incoming president and his or her administration understand the dynamics of hostage incidents and work to mitigate loss of life, damage to national prestige, and provision of truly damaging concessions.

GOALS, PRINCIPLES, AND ROLES IN HOSTAGE SITUATIONS

Terrorists who seize an embassy, theater, or hospital aim principally to discredit the national leadership of an adversary. By possessing hostages and potentially killing them over the international airwaves, terrorists seek to demonstrate that a government's leadership is impotent and incapable of defending its most important possession, i.e., the lives of its citizens. With the emergence of the suicidal tactics of Hezbollah, Hamas, al Qaeda, the Chechens, and the Liberation Tigers of Tamil Eelam, the management of these incidents became significantly more complex. To gain an appreciation for handling such situations, a brief description of players and roles follows. It provides the basics for understanding a standard barricade situation, including aircraft hijackings and other sieges.

Head of State: The president or prime minister whose government is confronted with an incident. Presidents usually have final decision-making authority in the handling of a terrorist incident. They should make known their counterterrorism policy immediately on entry into office and thereby ensure that all of those in the chain of command have guiding parameters to follow when making decisions during a crisis. It is critical that each person involved in the process of resolving an incident, from administrative help in the president's office to perimeter security at the incident site, know and understand the president's policy. The president is likely to have a small team of advisers to help him or her make key decisions.

National Crisis Committee: A committee of senior government officials with national security, defense, foreign affairs, intelligence, and homeland security credentials who will communicate recommendations to the president and maintain contact directly with an on-scene commander at a terrorist incident site. Members of the National Crisis Committee should be at the assistant secretary level and be career specialists with knowledge and experience in managing the assets that a government may need to employ during a crisis.

On-Scene Commander: The senior officer at the location closest to the incident who controls all forces involved in supporting the resolution of a crisis. As the old adage of crisis management goes, "Commanders never negotiate and negotiators never command." The on-scene commander never participates in direct negotiations with the terrorists. He or she always uses a trained negotiating team. The on-scene commander manages the negotiation team leader, the security team leader, the hostage rescue/assault team commander, the intelligence team leader, the communications team leader, the logistics/support team leader, and the public affairs/press team leader. The lead negotiator will keep the commander apprised of the terrorist group's demands. At the same time the on-scene commander will seek to reduce the number of hostages inside the barricade as much as possible to lessen casualties in the event of an assault. The on-scene commander should have the authority to conduct an assault without approval from the president and National Crisis Committee any time he believes that the terrorists are killing hostages inside the barricade or if the terrorists attempt an armed breakout.

Negotiation Team: Led by a lead negotiator, the negotiation team attempts to establish a channel of communication with the terrorists inside the barricaded space. The negotiators' goal is to establish a rapport with the terrorists and over time seek common ground to avoid the murder of hostages and interject reason into the situation. A negotiator should never say the word "no" to the hostage takers. If the terrorists set deadlines, the negotiators must try to talk them past those deadlines without the loss of life. The negotiator is an intermediary and must always seek higher approval.

Security Team: Two perimeters must be established around an incident site. One is an inner perimeter that contains the event and an armed security team, which also facilitates intelligence collection through visual observation. The second, outer perimeter, also armed, must be established to keep the curious, the press, and those who might want to support or reinforce the terrorists from gaining access to the site. The on-scene commander determines who is permitted inside the outer perimeter. From time to time, unwelcome officials seeking recognition will appear at an incident in order to raise their public profile. Fame seekers must be denied access to the incident scene by security forces.

Hostage Rescue/Assault Team: The hostage rescue/assault team leader must prepare his or her team for action from the moment an incident begins. The team's avenues of approach, cover, and concealment are the leader's primary concerns. Hostage rescue teams preparing to enter buildings should have mastered the most advanced breeching techniques. Breeching techniques require team members to find old buildings to train in, where they can practice tearing doors off their hinges or blasting open doors and walls without killing themselves or hostages inside a barricade. Hostage rescue teams preparing for an assault on an aircraft must practice on the type of aircraft that has been hijacked in order to understand its exact layout and potential obstacles. The danger of gaining forced access to an aircraft full of hostages and loaded with ten thousand gallons of highly flammable jet fuel cannot be overemphasized. In Malta in 1984, Egyptian forces in a rescue attempt used an explosive charge against an airliner and caused a fire that resulted in the deaths of many of the passengers they were trying to save.

Intelligence Team: The intelligence team provides information to the on-scene commander regarding the identities, capabilities, and intentions of the terrorists. The team members collect this intelligence from passenger manifests in the case of hijacked planes, boats, or trains, from the debriefing of released hostages, or from telescopic photos taken or voice analysis conducted during negotiations. Intelligence teams will use the full array of technical collection systems against terrorists and interface with national and international partners to provide the fullest possible level of understanding of the terrorists to the on-scene commander, National Crisis Committee, and president.

Communications Team: The communications team must establish multiple land lines to allow for direct uninhibited communication between the on-scene commander, the president, and the National Crisis Committee. Additionally, specific restricted telephone lines must be established that link the on-scene commander with the negotiation team, the security team, the hostage rescue/assault team, the intelligence team, the communications team, and the logistics/support team.

Logistics/Support Team: The logistics/support team establishes command posts and ensures that food, beds, computers, and other supplies are provided for crisis management staff. In 1986 a Pan Am flight was hijacked by a group of terrorists in Pakistan directed by Libyan president Muammar al-Kaddafi. The plane was taken while on the ground at Karachi's international airport, and the terrorists separated the passengers, placing a number of American citizens in business class. While the plane was sitting at the gate, it was hooked up to an auxiliary power unit (APU), which provided it with electricity. A laborer noticed the APU needed to be refueled so that it would not lose power and told those in command. But the command staff did not listen to him. When the APU finally ran out of fuel, the plane lost electricity and the lights went out. The terrorists believed that an assault was in progress and opened fire on the hostages, killing twenty of them. The failure to deal effectively with logistic and support functions in this case resulted in this significant loss of life.

Public Affairs/Press Team: At least twice a day the on-scene commander must have a public affairs spokesperson release information to the press that will meet the press's needs without compromising the incident's resolution in a manner favorable to the government. It is critical that the news cycles receive accurate input that discourages irresponsible stories, which might have a negative impact on the resolution of the crisis.

With the above descriptions of responsibilities one can gain an appreciation for the number of issues facing a national leader, an on-scene commander, and a crisis management staff when dealing with a hijacking or barricade situation. It is critical that neither the national leader nor the on-scene commander become directly involved in the negotiation process. Terrorists who are able to establish direct communication with a person in power will expect that their requests be acted on immediately. By using negotiators as intermediaries, a national leader and on-scene commander buy time. National leaders personally enter into the negotiating process almost always because they want to demonstrate their skill, power, and popularity. A national leader's direct involvement almost always results in the terrorists making demands that the leader cannot meet, which places hostages or national interests under even greater risk.

A U.S. president must be wary when incidents that affect U.S. interests take place on foreign soil or where the United States is denied access to the critical processes of resolution. Variables such as the country's internal politics and the direct intervention of other political players can have an adverse effect on a crisis situation.

I participated in a process where a foreign government worked hard to establish the mechanisms and personnel for command, security, intelligence, and hostage negotiators. But when a hostage situation developed at the nation's parliament, the third-ranking official in the country, with responsibility over law enforcement forces, refused to allow those trained for the crisis to manage it. The third-ranking official was able to convince his president that he had things in order. That senior official sent in his own negotiators to deal with a man who had strapped explosives to himself. One hour after the official's negotiators arrived, other security personnel attempted an unapproved and uncoordinated effort to disarm the man. The attempt failed and the explosives detonated, killing and injuring many. Political incompetence and a refusal to make use of the government's trained personnel led to this disaster. The incompetent third-ranking political figure and an uninformed press blamed the security forces.

CONTAINMENT

Containment is critical in any aircraft hijacking or barricade situation. If an aircraft is seized at an airport while on the ground, every measure must be made to ensure that the aircraft does not take off. In the United States, this is standard practice. In some countries abroad it is not. When U.S. aircraft or U.S. citizens are involved in a hostage crisis, a president must call foreign counterparts to explain the importance of containing the situation. The president cannot assume that a foreign head of state will function competently in a crisis: In 1985, Hezbollah terrorists hijacked TWA Flight 847 and landed it in Beirut, where they murdered U.S. Navy diver Robert Dean Stethem and then unloaded the passengers into terrorist-held neighborhoods. The North Koreans allowed numerous aircraft hijacked by the terrorist group known as the Japanese Red Army to land in North Korea in the 1970s and then provided sanctuary to the JRA hijackers in Pyongyang. An Air India flight hijacked out of Nepal in 1998 landed in Taliban-controlled Afghanistan, where Kashmiri terrorists pressured the Indian government to release Islamic terrorists held in Indian prisons. Hijacked aircraft cannot be permitted to hopscotch their way around the world en route to terrorist safe havens, and terrorists who have created a barricade situation should not be permitted to move via vehicles with their hostages out of an airport into an urban area or across an international border.

RESCUE EFFORTS

The United States and its allies have made advancements in the tactics, technology, and execution of hostage rescue since the 1970s. Rescues for hijacking and barricade situations within the United States are made by the FBI's Hostage Rescue Team or a SWAT team from one of the major U.S. metropolitan areas. If a crisis situation abroad involves a significant number of U.S. hostages, the U.S. Army's Delta Force receives the rescue mission. Presidents must understand that hostage rescues are especially deadly and difficult outside U.S. borders and that they cannot necessarily expect a rescue force, American or foreign, to attempt a rescue using nonlethal means. In planning for the April 1980 rescue of American hostages held in Tehran, President Carter placed numerous limitations on the team planning the assault and rescue. Plans for the mission involving the seizure of a small paved airfield guarded by an Iranian staff of five to seven soldiers were scrapped because President

Carter didn't want anyone killed. He additionally ordered the force to bring stun grenades for use in the event they met resistance from the population of Tehran. President Carter's desire that the rescue mission avoid casualties was humane and decent yet naive. Ultimately his naivete contributed to the mission's failure. In this case the president lacked an understanding of his adversaries, the conflict, and crisis management in general.

As of 2007, only a few dozen countries in the world are capable of successfully resolving a major hijacking or barricade situation. To get it right, national leaders must understand the above principles and make their countries invest in a capability and command structure that can adequately respond to the challenges. Frequently countries build their capability bit by bit as they face an ongoing crisis. In the process they make errors that cost lives and national prestige, and this only encourages terrorists to strike again.

PRESIDENTIAL DECISION-MAKING IN A CRISIS

In a crisis a president will be faced with numerous decisions. The most critical of these decisions should be made only after he or she has been updated by his or her closest advisers, the National Crisis Committee, and the American official closest to the scene. If the event has occurred in the United States, the president should speak directly with the FBI on-scene commander regarding what is transpiring on the ground before making any decisions. Similarly, if the event has occurred abroad, the president should call the U.S. ambassador and the CIA station chief. A president should seek real-time information about conditions at the scene, if and when a presidential decision is to be made.

COMBAT COUNTERTERRORISM

The United States will likely have combat forces on the ground in Afghanistan and Iraq for the next several years as part of the ongoing battle in the Islamic world between those who believe Islam can coexist with efforts to establish secular forms of representative government and those who seek theocratic Islamic rule.* As

---

* Zeyno Baran, "Fighting the War of Ideas," *Foreign Affairs* 84, no. 6 (November–December 2005).

it did during the Cold War, the United States must stand with those who desire secular, representative government prepared to respect fundamental human rights and not with the Islamic theocracies, which seem to have replaced communist governments as the world's dark, intolerant force. The large and active infrastructure of religious education in the Islamic world, which teaches anti-U.S./anti-Western values, only guarantees that many more will be prepared to employ terrorist attacks against U.S. forces and Muslims pursuing secular government in the coming years.

In the course of ongoing conflicts like the one America currently faces, it is not only important to develop sources within insurgent and terrorist groups but to fully exploit those sources. Exploiting sources will enable our forces to identify and neutralize terrorist group leaders and members. What has worked best in the past is fusing the CIA's HUMINT and military operators with U.S. military strike capability so that intelligence may be immediately employed in the pursuit of terrorist leaders and their key lieutenants. The CIA collects, documents, and disseminates its intelligence with incredible speed.

When a manhunt against a key terrorist leader such as Abu Musab al-Zarqawi, the leader of al Qaeda in Iraq, is under way, it is critical for commanders to have immediate and continuing access to intelligence collection planning sessions. Access will allow a commander to be in the optimal position to anticipate and prepare action to achieve favorable goals. Embedding military officers in CIA field elements close to or on the battlefield allows a commander to keep apace of smaller, more nimble operational elements and to fully exploit opportunities that its presence and operations may create.

Prior to 2001, the CIA and military did not embed personnel in one another's operations. It is important that this practice of fusing the two capabilities continues. Tactics established during wartime are frequently dismantled when stability or peace is achieved: senior CIA and military officers who forged positive professional and personal relationships during the war on terrorism may be transferred or replaced by others who fail to maintain intimate coordination and cooperation. I witnessed this failure in Afghanistan in 2007–2008. The relationship between the intelligence community and the military was cooperative in some areas and almost nonexistent in others. This is simply not beneficial.

RETAINING THE CIA'S PARAMILITARY CAPABILITY

In the years immediately following September 11, 2001, numerous debates about how to improve our intelligence and better coordinate our responses to that intelligence were conducted. As part of this debate the issue of stripping the CIA of paramilitary capability in favor of placing this capability under the Department of Defense's authority was made and championed by a number of those at the Pentagon. The U.S. armed forces, which number over 1.5 million men and women, have thousands of combat aircraft, hundreds of ships, and a dozen or so divisions of combat troops, still believed it was critical to seize control of the CIA's Special Activities Division, which is no more than a few hundred officers. The Special Activities Division is not an alternative Delta Force, or a hostage rescue team. It is a group of intelligence professionals that allows the CIA to conduct intelligence operations in the most dangerous parts of the world. Its officers have both classic intelligence backgrounds and special operations backgrounds.

In this case, the Pentagon was seeking not to improve its own capability but to strip the intelligence community of its capability. As discussed in chapter 3, the CIA conducts covert action around the world at the president's direction and with the knowledge of Congress. Stripping the CIA of its paramilitary capability would significantly damage the agency's covert action capabilities and necessitate that the U.S. military enter this arena on a broader scale. This in turn would reduce congressional oversight.

It is certain that some in the Defense Department will continue to lobby to strip the CIA of its paramilitary capability as the war on terrorism progresses. A future president must understand that the United States found success in Afghanistan in 2001 because the CIA had paramilitary capability. Do not strip the CIA of its paramilitary capability.

RETAINING THE CIA'S CLANDESTINE SERVICE

Recently, some politicians have called for the dissolution of the CIA's Clandestine Service in favor of creating a new intelligence organization. In his book *Fixing Intelligence*, the former director of the National Security Agency, Gen. William Odom, made clear his opinion about CIA operations officers who deal with sources and operational issues: he noted that they had "culture problems," implying he believes they did not tell the truth. General Odom goes on to say that any new organization that takes the Clandestine Service's place should be imbued with the values taught in the precommissioning training of military officers.

General Odom fails to note that a large percentage of the CIA's Clandestine Service has previous military service. A number of CIA officers have sacrificed their lives in operations designed to provide intelligence to the president in order to save American lives. In his failure to acknowledge these points, General Odom reveals his naivete regarding the CIA's Clandestine Service. An incoming president must recognize that many who will advise him or her on the workings of the intelligence community have little to no practical experience with HUMINT and may direct the president with the intention of settling old political scores.

The press is full of stories about how the CIA failed to accomplish certain tasks and blundered in others. What these articles overlook is the fact that on a daily basis CIA operations officers conduct remarkable operations advancing U.S. interests and supporting allied governments to save hundreds if not thousands of lives. CIA officers prefer to be called incompetent by the press and angry politicians than to reveal their good coverage of a difficult or dangerous target or situation. Thus they protect their sources and methods. If a president believes significant changes are needed to advance his or her foreign intelligence (FI) needs, then adjustments in clandestine collection should be made within the CIA's current Clandestine Service. The complete dismantling of the CIA's collection capability would place Americans unnecessarily at risk during this time of global unrest.

CRITICAL POINTS

- Military HUMINT would benefit from the guidance of a senior CIA operations officer. The military has demonstrated an inability to address basic HUMINT problems.

- Commanders never negotiate, and negotiators never command. A president should never permit him- or herself to be personally drawn into negotiations with terrorists. He or she should follow the standard crisis management principles and delegate tasks as necessary to the on-scene commander.

- In a crisis, a commander in chief should not hesitate to communicate directly with an on-scene commander or ambassador to learn the situation on the ground in real time before making a critical decision.

- Deparment of Defense efforts to strip the CIA of its paramilitary capability do not serve the nation's interests.

- The CIA must be retained as the principle organization that conducts FI collection.

- A president needs to participate actively in the process of containing international aircraft hijackings. He or she should call on allied leaders to support denying such aircraft freedom of movement.

6. LANGUAGE SKILLS:

PREPARING FOR TOMORROW TODAY

In the course of U.S. military operations in Afghanistan and Iraq, the world has seen American strength, our ability to deploy forces to far corners of the planet, and the incredible lethality of our combined arms operations. These operations have also highlighted the difficulty of conducting counterinsurgency against enemies with nearby sanctuary and fielding a sufficient number of officers and men with the requisite linguistic and cultural knowledge. In our efforts in both Afghanistan and Iraq, ensuring delivery of our message of freedom of opportunity and self-government is critical. Specifically, we need to ensure that the native populations understand that we are working to reestablish order and security and to provide them with a representative government reflective of their culture and values. To deliver this message, and do so many other things, we need many more Farsi and Arab speakers than we have today. Language skills are critical to operating effectively in any foreign culture.

LANGUAGE SKILLS AND THE CIA

Considering that terrorists and small subnational groups that communicate in obscure languages may plan and execute significant attacks on the United States in the future, the CIA needs to staff linguists. Thus far the agency has failed to recognize and adequately address the significant shortage of critical language skills among its officers. To do nothing about the dearth in agency linguists during the current war on terrorism is a failure of leadership that extends to the White House.

A president interested in the defense of the United States and the health of the Clandestine Service needs to ask, What percentage of case officers in the field assigned to countries where the United States is currently involved in combat operations speak the local language? One would assume that those countries where U.S. soldiers are fighting and dying would receive the highest allotment in case officers with relevant language skills, but this is not the case.

I have developed the following scale to grade the CIA's success in hiring, training, and fielding appropriately trained case officers in Afghanistan, Iraq, and other Muslim and Arabic countries. To use the scale, the CIA must provide the exact number of operations officers on the ground in the assigned countries with Arabic or Farsi/Dari and Pashto language skills as well as the officers' language proficiency scores. The number must not be inflated by the agency's future plans to assign officers with relevant language skills, and it must not include the number of translators on the ground. Translators are not case officers.

60 percent of case officers have functional language ability = Outstanding

50 percent of case officers have functional language ability = Excellent

40 percent of case officers have functional language ability = Good

30 percent of case officers have functional language ability = Fair

20 percent of case officers have functional language ability = Poor

10 percent of case officers have functional language ability = Failure

5 percent of case officers have functional language ability = Disgraceful

The CIA's score on this scale will be troubling.

All components of the U.S. government are short of qualified Arabic-, Pashto-, and Farsi/Dari-speaking officers, be they native-born speakers or trained linguists. To meet the challenges of the current conflict between the United States and the Islamic jihadists, we must begin training diplomats, intelligence officers, soldiers, and aid workers in the languages and customs of the Islamic world.

To begin, we must recognize that the university language programs in the United States do not sufficiently prepare individuals to meet the challenges of the conflicts in the Middle East and South Asia. I recommend that the federal government create a Center for Middle Eastern Studies in a location in the United States that already has a heavy concentration of native Arabic speakers. At least one million Arab Americans live in the greater Detroit area; the heaviest concentration of this population lives and works in Dearborn, Michigan. This large population of Arab Americans, many with cultural and religious ties to the Middle East, could easily provide the expertise and manpower needed to create a college-accredited institute that could train between one hundred and five hundred people a year in Arabic and other critical Middle Eastern languages such as Farsi, Dari, Urdu, and Pashto. Courses in Middle Eastern history, economics, and culture should also be part of the program. Detroit has suffered economically in recent decades and would benefit from the investment involved in creating the institution. Thus Dearborn would be an optimal venue for this effort at advancing our national security goals.

LANGUAGE SKILLS AT THE DEFENSE DEPARTMENT

The British Empire at one point covered 40 percent of the world, including India, Pakistan, Nigeria, Hong Kong, Australia, and Fiji. One of the keys to imperial British success was a well-trained officer corps with significant linguistic ability. Most of the officers in the British Indian Army were expected to learn to give orders in their troops' native language and were given handsome bonuses to be fluent in those languages. British officers were expected to operate in extremely isolated areas such as Waziristan, Pakistan, with locally recruited troops. Their knowledge of local languages and customs were crucial to their successes. The U.S. military must follow the British example and stress linguistic ability.

The U.S. Department of Defense maintains four military academies, including the U.S. Military Academy at West Point, New York, for the army; the U.S. Naval Academy in Annapolis, Maryland, for the navy and Marine Corps; the U.S. Air Force Academy in Colorado Springs, Colorado; and the Coast Guard Academy in New

London, Connecticut. At present at least fifteen thousand total cadets are in training at these institutions, preparing to become officers in the U.S. armed forces. What these academies need is a mandatory four-year program in Middle Eastern languages for every cadet. At least half of the graduating cadets at West Point will be sent to Iraq or Afghanistan to lead troops on the ground within two years. Only a small percentage of these cadets will have studied Arabic, Dari, or Pashto while at the academy, and an even smaller number will have operational capacity in the language. I strongly recommend altering the curriculum at West Point and the other military academies to ensure that for four years at least half of these cadets receive one hour a day of a Middle Eastern language course geared to enhancing performance of duties under the conditions that they will face in Iraq and Afghanistan.

Studying psychology, sociology, and American literature are all worthwhile pursuits in developing knowledge of the world. However, those courses of study do little to aid a second lieutenant leading a platoon of soldiers into a hostile town so that they can determine friend from foe. Speaking the natives' language will increase the likelihood that such young officers can conduct their missions successfully and help reduce the loss of men and women under their command. Because the military has not yet made the study of Middle Eastern languages compulsory curriculum at its academies, the president as commander in chief should order that this be done.

At least 50 percent of the thousands of other students who attend college on U.S. Military Reserve Officer Training Corps (ROTC) scholarships should also be required to take Middle Eastern language courses. This should include yearlong study abroad programs in which the students are encouraged to study one of the key languages at a university in the Middle East.

Thousands of civilian intelligence officers work for the Department of Defense. Any of these officers who could be assigned to the field at some point in their careers should be encouraged to learn Arabic, Farsi/Dari, or Pashto. Once they have graduated from this language training, they should have a special identifier that marks them as a linguist for the rest of their careers.

Having thousands of Arabic or Farsi linguists would make a huge difference in the global war on terrorism. In the 1980s the United States won the war in El Salvador in part because it had tens of thousands of Spanish speakers in the U.S. Army who could communicate with natives on the ground. This made a huge difference on our ability to function in that society.

Finally, it must be noted that during the past few years, at a time when our need for Arabic linguists has been dire, a number of Arabic speakers have been discharged from the armed forces because it was learned that they were either gay or lesbian servicemembers. Opponents of allowing gays and lesbians in the military argue that the presence of these people will damage morale. What is more damaging to unit morale, however, is the deaths of soldiers, marines, airmen, and sailors that America has suffered because our troops lack sufficient language skills. When Arabic- or Farsi-speaking men and women are removed from duty, we must rely on interpreters whose loyalties are suspect. In fact, local national interpreters have frequently had to be removed from their positions because they reported information to jihadists and insurgents. Gays and lesbians have served in the FBI and CIA openly with little to no accompanying drop in morale. Simply put, we need every man and woman willing to step forward in this fight, regardless of sexual orientation. It is time to lift the ban on gays and lesbians in the U.S. armed forces.

CRITICAL POINTS

- Establish a federal institute for Middle Eastern studies in Dearborn, Michigan, to take advantage of the large Arab-American population whose help we need in the war on terrorism.

- The president must order that all those studying at U.S. military academies study a Middle Eastern language for all four years of their study.

- At least 50 percent of students on ROTC scholarships should be required to take part in an intensive Middle Eastern language program, which should include a year-long study abroad program in the Middle East.

- Every man and woman, regardless of sexual orientation, should be permitted to serve in the U.S. armed forces. As this issue relates to our shortage of linguists, strategic necessity intersects with constitutional fairness.

7. TERRORIST FINANCES AND THE INTERNET

TERRORIST FINANCES

Much is said and written about efforts to block terrorist finances. The important thing to keep in mind is that in some cases these measures are extremely useful and in others they have little or no effect. Terrorist financing has been best controlled by measures that have blocked the large streams of cash coming out of Saudi Arabia to the array of nonprofit Islamic charities that facilitated the movement of people and resources in support of the worldwide jihadist movement. Organizations such as al-Haramain Islamic Foundation and the World Assembly of Muslim Youth (WAMY) have provided cover for terrorist cells' recruiting and organizing efforts in various countries across the globe. Congress has passed legislation that allows the U.S. Treasury Department to take punitive measures against institutions that facilitate banking privileges for nongovernmental organizations (NGOs) associated with jihadists. This legislation has choked off the finances of NGOs that have served as front organizations for terrorist groups and further reduced the capacity of those NGOs to recruit, organize, and fund terrorist activities.

The same legal mechanisms have proved devastating against the Hamas government in the Palestinian Authority. Hamas, which won the 2006 parliamentary election in the Palestinian territories, openly employs suicide bombers against the civilian population of Israel and has, as part of its charter, called for the destruction of the Jewish state, which it plans to replace with an Islamic fundamentalist government. U.S. legislation was designed to compel Treasury Department banking sanctions against anyone who facilitated transactions with a terrorist organization. These sanctions left the

Hamas-led Palestinian Authority in Gaza cut off from economic aid from the United States and European Union and led to the Palestinian Authority's failure to meet the salary needs of its 186,000 government employees. Until Hamas accepts Israel's right to exist and halts the use of suicide bombers and other terrorists, these tools should continue to be used against Hamas.

Of greater concern is an informal financial system, first created in South Asia and existing outside the regulated international financial system, known as *hawala* or *hundi*. In the hawala system, individual money men, primarily in the Middle East, South Asia, Africa, and East Asia, facilitate transfers of cash between parties that are not taxed, recorded, or registered by governments or regulatory bodies. These informal networks remain largely outside government control, and monitoring them presents a significant challenge to closing terrorist financial exchanges.* For example, a *hawaladar*, that is, a person who runs a hawala, in Dallas, Texas, could use his telephone or fax machine to move funds generated by legitimate means, without the knowledge of authorities, to a counterpart in the Gaza Strip who in turn could pass the money to Hamas for an attack on Israel. In this example, the two cooperating hawaladars would make a profit by charging a transaction fee and by bypassing official exchange rates. Operating outside of a regulatory system, hawaladars are free to set their own exchange rates when they change the original remittance—in this example the U.S. dollar—to a payout in a second currency—that used by Hamas. Investigating hawala transactions is difficult because in many cases this informal system either allows multiple transactions to be merged together or involves the passage of funds through countries where law enforcement is virtually nonexistent. Thus reconstructing transactions in subsequent investigations is tricky. These investigations are manpower intensive and costly.

THE INTERNET

The Internet plays two primary roles for those involved in terrorism: First, propaganda is as important to today's terrorists as

---

* "Dirty Money: Tracing the Misuse of Hawala Networks," *Jane's Intelligence Review*, February 13, 2008.

their hidden financial networks are. Just as Thomas Paine urged Americans to revolt in his 1776 pamphlet *Common Sense*, Islamic jihadists use propaganda to spread their message and call others to action. Second, the Internet provides a fast, accurate, and, if employed cleverly, secure means of communication among terrorists. Secure clandestine communication is critical to any terrorist planning, and the Internet is the communication tool of choice among numerous terrorist groups.

The Internet, however, is not as effective as some would have us believe when it comes to actually recruiting and training terrorists. Following both the 2004 Madrid and 2005 London bombings of mass transit systems, the media was full of stories about self-forming terrorist groups and the impact of the Internet. In the case of the Madrid bombings, Judge Juan del Olmo found "local cells of Islamic extremists inspired through the Internet" guilty of the attacks—not better known North African terrorist groups such as Groupe Islamique Armé (GIA) or the Moroccan Islamic Combatant Group. Given the scale of the operation—ten improvised explosive devices detonated against local trains resulting in 191 dead and 1,755 injured—completely ruling out al Qaeda involvement is difficult, especially because the principal terrorists blew themselves up in an apartment building rather than face capture. Similar conjecture that a local extremist group conducted the London suicide bombings was shown to be false in 2006 when al Qaeda released a video of the group's leader, Mohammad Sidique Khan, discussing his plan for the suicide attack. Al Qaeda's number two, Ayman al-Zawahiri, appeared on the video immediately following Khan. The video proved that Khan had personal contact with and training from al Qaeda and that his group's activities were not locally inspired but rather coordinated and directed by al Qaeda from the Afghan-Pakistani border region.

The seventeen suspected terrorists arrested in Toronto and the seven arrested in Miami in 2006, in contrast, were clearly unprofessional self-starters. They were identified and arrested well before they had the means to carry out their planned attacks. These men were inspired by reports and propaganda they found in the media, but their cases only prove that the Internet cannot provide the leadership and mentoring needed to form and manage successful clandestine actions.

In the vast majority of significant terrorist attacks, a leader who has had indoctrination and training emerges to share his knowledge with locally recruited members. The key to counterterrorist success is early identification of this experienced terrorist member. With this leadership, a small, newly established group consisting of a handful of members with moderately good-paying jobs and access to technology can pool their money and resources together in order to construct and deliver an attack. The first attack on the World Trade Center by Ramzi Yusuf and his cohorts and Timothy McVeigh's attack on the Alfred P. Murrah Federal Building in Oklahoma City each cost less than twenty-five thousand dollars. Because significant resources are not always required for a terrorist to do great harm, we need the FBI to conduct human source intelligence operations in each of the key metropolitan areas of the United States. Human penetrations are the only way to go after local cells.

CRITICAL POINTS

- A good number of terrorist groups move their funds via the informal hawala system, and investigating these systems requires extensive manpower and resources.

- Terrorism is cheap; small groups operating on their own can self-fund deadly endeavors. Supercomputers and reviewing bank transactions will not help authorities in cases of self-financed groups.

8. THE FREEDOM CORPS

As I write this book, U.S. forces are in Iraq fighting a deadly combination of jihadists, holdover Baathists, al Qaeda, and Iranian-sponsored special groups. At the same time, in Afghanistan, U.S. forces are facing the Taliban, al Qaeda, and other anticoalition militants. In both places, no immediate end to combat operations is in sight.

The conflict we are engaged in is against a group whose belief system is characterized by the seventh-century philosophy of Islam. Somalia's Islamic Courts government, driven from Mogadishu by the Ethiopians in late 2006, claimed to represent this oppressive ideology; so do the Taliban and al Qaeda. Those who want this kind of seventh-century Islamic rule provide support and sanctuary to America's enemies, i.e., governments open in declaring their hostility to the United States.

America's battle with Islamic jihadists is certain to be a long war. In addition to continuing the military efforts in Iraq and Afghanistan, we must employ political and economic policies demonstrating competence and compassion and provide for basic security in places where we intervene. This must be done by supporting the population's stake in their future, and we must be careful not to alienate the host populations in this process. The cost of the ongoing effort has already been high in terms of blood and treasure. It is therefore paramount we think creatively and establish a new formula increasing our effectiveness on the ground while simultaneously reducing our losses and costs.

BRIEF OVERVIEW OF SURROGATE FORCES

For more than a century the British employed foreign forces, which fought under British officers, to pursue Britain's interests. A brief look at the creation and use of one of these forces, the British

Gurkhas, is instructive. After a costly entry into Nepal in the 1814–16 Gurkha War, the British were held to a stalemate by the forces of King Shah of Gurkha. A peace treaty was signed in which the British promised not to return to Nepalese soil with force and King Shah promised to allow Britain to recruit soldiers from his kingdom. Thus, the British Gurkhas were born.

The Gurkhas remained loyal during the Indian Mutiny of 1857 and saw action during both world wars and in the Falklands War, and they are part of the current British contingent of forces in Afghanistan's southern provinces. British officers command these enlisted Gurkha soldiers and noncommissioned officers, who serve for up to fifteen years, at which point they become eligible for retirement. India has maintained its own Gurkha regiments since independence from Britain in 1947. Under the same model, these Nepali soldiers are recruited in Nepal and then led on the field by Indian officers as part of the Indian army.[*]

Similar is the French Foreign Legion, a force commanded by the finest French military officers and comprised of foreigners from around the world. Applicants to the legion are accepted as long as they are not wanted for murder. All legionnaires receive a name change and after five years are eligible for French citizenship. The French Foreign Legion is romanticized in many Hollywood movies and continues to serve France in deployments in the most dangerous and difficult conflicts around the world.

The United States also has used surrogate forces. The Philippine Scouts were a military unit based in the Philippines from 1900 to 1946. The scouts, numbering 11,000, were led by U.S. officers and Filipino graduates of West Point and fought in World War II. At one point during the Vietnam War, U.S. soldiers from the 5th Special Forces Group commanded troops comprised of Montagnard tribesmen, Nung (ethnic Chinese) soldiers, and Cambodians. In Laos, CIA paramilitary officers commanded units comprised of Hmong tribesmen and Thai troops.

THE FREEDOM CORPS

To face the current international situation, I recommend that

---

[*] Byron Farwell, *The Gurkhas* (New York: Norton, 1984).

the United States establish a surrogate corps of light infantry, combat engineers, and military police (totaling roughly twenty thousand men and women) called the Freedom Corps. This group should be led by U.S. officers and consist primarily of enlisted men and women from the Islamic world. The majority of the enlisted soldiers serving as part of this force should be native Arabic, Farsi/Dari, Pashto, Uzbek, and Somali speakers. The corps should be trained and led by American servicemen and women primarily for the mission of counterinsurgency.

As an incentive for a multiyear assignment, U.S. officers should serve with the Freedom Corps at the next highest rank and, after three to four years of service, return with that rank to the U.S. armed forces. Senior U.S. noncommissioned officers (E-7s, E-8s, and E-9s) and senior warrant officers would be able to enter the Freedom Corps as officers up to the rank of captain. Senior enlisted and warrant officers should not return to the regular armed forces but rather should retire with the grade they achieved in the Freedom Corps.

Those foreign enlisted and noncommissioned officers selected for entry and service in the Freedom Corps should receive basic and advanced infantry training. The most talented applicants should be given political agent positions. Large areas in Afghanistan fall outside government control, and these political agents would be useful in establishing links to communities in previously ungoverned areas. Freedom Corps members would be eligible for U.S. permanent residence status, a Green Card, after five years. Women should be recruited not for combat functions but for intelligence and other support disciplines. After an initial five-year enlistment, a soldier in the Freedom Corps should be permitted to reenlist or immigrate to the United States. The highest performers should be eligible for a direct transfer into the U.S. armed forces. Because the United States will never be able to field enough native speakers of Middle Eastern and East Asian languages to support intelligence and special ops activities, the Freedom Corps is necessary to provide the U.S. military with a pipeline to those skills.

The benefits of creating such a force are significant. A Muslim force working among Islamic populations is much more likely to engender the needed support to achieve victory against established insurgencies. When the corps soldiers communicate with a local population they will use a common language. The soldiers will attend mosques and pray with the local population. They will be the vanguard of a larger, distinctly Islamic force alleviating the feeling of foreign occupation. Those joining the force will receive training and education about America and the world that they have never before been afforded. An Islamic force led by U.S. personnel would be potent.

The salaries for Freedom Corps soldiers should be from USD $750 to $1,000 per month. This recommended level would lift the soldiers and their families out of poverty and simultaneously cut our own expenses for training and deploying U.S. forces, which are currently much higher. Housing, training, maintaining, feeding, and arming this force would cost significantly less than U.S. force requirements. The corps should enlist only single men and women. After five years of service, these soldiers should be permitted to marry and support a family.

Clearly, this idea will garner some opposition. Some in the U.S. military will view this as an encroachment on their area of responsibility and will claim this idea is inconsistent with U.S. military values and history. Those in the Islamic world who oppose the United States will cry foul. How dare the United States expose its values and politics to Muslims?! People from around the world will scream that this is yet more proof that America is pursuing an empire. But, as Machiavelli wrote in *The Prince*, "Nothing is more dangerous or difficult than introducing a new order of things."

The Freedom Corps has the potential to improve U.S. power, influence, and capability throughout the Islamic world. Many who truly want a chance for freedom and advancement will come to us. Let them come, and fight alongside us; let us together change the dynamics of the war against Islamic jihadists. The Afghanistan government should be approached and asked for permission to establish the Freedom Corps on its soil. Battalion-sized elements should be established along ethnic and linguistic lines. U.S. officers should be required to learn their soldiers' native language, and the soldiers should all receive English language training so that English can be established as the corps' link language.

THE DEVELOPMENT OF THE CORPS

The following isn't designed to be comprehensive but rather a broad-brush overview of topics relevant to the Freedom Corps. Sub-topics will be formulated by people who have developed similar forces in the past. Remember that the primary purpose of the Freedom Corps is to fight a counterinsurgency.

The Freedom Corps must be able to govern itself with its own version of the Uniform Code of Military Justice (UCMJ). The organizational structure should support effective communication. Organizational funding should be set at a level appropriate to maximize the combination of fundamental soldiering, intelligence, and appropriate basic technologies.

Rules of engagement (ROE) should be set when and where the enemy is restricted and the Freedom Corps can execute missions effectively. When not properly planned, ROE can minimize production capacity and counteract functionality; less restriction tends to increase results. The Freedom Corps commander should report to the assistant secretary of defense for special operations and low intensity conflict (ASD/SOLIC).

Training areas must be constructed in a timely manner to facilitate organization and keeping training time to a minimum. Bear in mind that it may be difficult to find locations to train soldiers in a war-torn area and that training sites will hold only a limited number of students at a time.

CRITICAL POINT

- A new force is necessary to face the challenges presented by Islamic jihadists. A Freedom Corps, staffed primarily with Muslims, will be a potent response to this challenge.

9. INTELLIGENCE AND FORCE LEVELS IN COUNTER- INSURGENCY OPERATIONS

*T*HE U.S. MILITARY AND COUNTERINSURGENCY

he U.S. Army/Marine Corps Counterinsurgency Field Manual, authored by Gen. David H. Petraeus, Lt. Gen. James F. Amos, and Lt. Col. John Nagl with the support of a number of others in uniform, provides a broad study of counterinsurgency and is an invaluable book. The manual acknowledges three significant works on the subject: *Counterinsurgency Warfare: Theory and Practice* by David Galula, "Battle Lessons: What Generals Don't Know" by Dan Baum, and *Defeating Communist Insurgency: The Lessons of Malaya and Vietnam* by Sir Robert Thompson.

The chapter from the manual of greatest interest here is about counterinsurgency and intelligence. It begins, "The ultimate success or failure of the mission (counterinsurgency) depends on the effectiveness of the intelligence effort." In all fairness, the U.S. military's handling of technology in the conduct of intelligence collection, be it signals intelligence or aerial reconnaissance, is impressive at both the brigade and battalion levels. U.S. servicemen and women have dedicated themselves to becoming masters of these disciplines. Unfortunately, they have failed to maintain their human intelligence capability. Layers of bureaucracy and the imposition of excessive regulations on HCTs has allowed the armed forces' HUMINT capacity to atrophy. Human intelligence is inexpensive, simple, and must be used to complement technical coverage.

The generally accepted ratio for protection in an insurgency is twenty counterinsurgents (security forces) for every one thousand citizens. Thus, the Afghan population—21 million citizens—requires 400,000 counterinsurgent forces to maintain security and separate the insurgents from the population. But, in Afghanistan the insurgency is concentrated in the east and south and affects 10 million of the country's total population. Thus, a more realistic number of security and counterinsurgent forces, according to the accepted ratio, is 200,000.

The reality of the Afghan situation is instructive. Coalition forces in Afghanistan equal 60,000. The Afghan National Army and Afghan National Police number roughly 70,000 and 50,000, respectively. Consider for a moment that half of the coalition forces are concentrated in the country's capital, Kabul. When you take location, self-imposed limitations forbidding the deployment of some coalition partners into combat areas, and the Afghan National Police's lack of training and resources, the true ratio of available forces for this counterinsurgency mission is further reduced. The math does not bode well. Because so few counterinsurgents are available to the population, success in this case is even more dependent on the successful collection of intelligence about our adversaries' plans and intentions.

A critical component of the effort and focus of U.S. forces in Afghanistan should be the development of joint U.S.-Afghan intelligence teams. Currently U.S. teams consist mostly of young white men with only a high school education, no local language ability, and limited cultural knowledge. Their goal is to acquire sources from among the population with the aim of penetrating insurgent groups. The U.S. military HCTs have had success establishing contact with local citizens, who report on what they see and hear in their villages. Though this contact is useful, it does not support the much-needed penetration of jihadist and terrorist groups.

Highly trained and skilled Defense Department case officers are stationed in the Afghan theater, but these officers are in Kabul, away from the fight. The truth is very few individuals with the requisite language and operational skills who can provide the level of human intelligence that the U.S. military needs to sufficiently advance our counterinsurgency efforts are actually present in Afghanistan today.

The answer to the problem of human intelligence collection lies in host nation integration, i.e., a joint human intelligence effort. *The Counterinsurgency Field Manual* addresses this subject with words of caution, warning of the risks associated with working with host country national intelligence units. It seems that the manual misses a couple critical points: because local nationals speak the natives' language, they can go where westerners cannot, and they have existing networks of social and professional contacts, which they have developed over their lifetimes. These advantages must be fully exploited to achieve operational success. In the Afghan theater the U.S. armed forces must launch a major joint U.S.-Afghan initiative, funded, trained, and led by the United States. The joint intelligence teams will be able to move among the population, identify the enemy, and penetrate enemy cells and networks. An effort executed broadly across contested regions of Afghanistan would alter the conflict and return the initiative to the United States and the coalition.

General Petraeus and his team of writers are biased against host nation integration of intelligence efforts because of their experience of working with Iraqi security forces, which have been penetrated by insurgents, Baathists, and terrorists. The difficulties American soldiers experienced in Iraq were and continue to be related to the insufficient vetting of Iraqi intelligence and security force personnel caused by the U.S. government's rush to legitimize Iraq as a functioning democracy.

DEFINING INSURGENCY

An insurgency is a protracted struggle by one or more armed groups that employ violence with the goal of overthrowing an existing political order. More simply, it is a campaign aimed at seizing political power. The term *insurgency* denotes a widespread organization of armed fighters and advanced political organization based on a common goal or ideology. Terrorism, for point of reference, is more accurately defined as premeditated, politically motivated violence perpetrated against noncombatant targets by subnational groups or clandestine agents.[1]

A president must understand that an insurgency is not a fight for strategic targets, though insurgents may attack such targets. It is also not a fight for land, though insurgents may seize territory. An insurgency is a fight for control of the population.[2] During the Vietnam War, it was popular in the United States to say Americans were fighting for the hearts and minds of the South Vietnamese population. The words *hearts and minds*, however, gave the false sense that the war was simply a popularity contest. Nothing could be farther from the truth. As David Galula noted in the early 1960s, counterinsurgency "is about the systematic employment of military, security, intelligence, and political assets in order to break the insurgents' contact and control of the population." And, in fact, many of the steps needed for the counterinsurgent to achieve victory will not be popular with the host population. It is important to understand that historically it has taken eight to ten years to defeat an insurgency.

Insurgents will use raw violence to intimidate the population into providing support to their effort, or at least into remaining neutral. The insurgents will torture and murder those cooperating with existing authorities as a means to establish control over the population. The population will not love the insurgents. They will cooperate with the insurgents out of fear for themselves and their families. The insurgents will gradually impress larger and larger percentages of the population into service. To achieve victory, a counterinsurgent force must have its forces out defending the population, not locked down safely on bases while the insurgency subjugates and punishes the people.

---

[1] Paul Pillar, *Terrorism and U.S. Foreign Policy* (Washington, DC: Brookings Institution Press, 2001).

[2] David Galula, *Counterinsurgency Warfare: Theory and Practice* (New York: Praeger, 1964).

EFFECTIVE COUNTERINSURGENCY

Combating an insurgency requires early recognition of the insurgency's formation and the early deployment of forces to counteract the insurgents' efforts. Counterinsurgency operations are different from normal conventional combat operations. Conventional combat operations involve overwhelming force and firepower. Combating an insurgency requires physically denying the insurgents access to the population. Well thought-out intelligence collection and social organization are necessities.

Manpower: In the execution of counterinsurgency operations, highly mobile light infantry, combat engineers, and military police should make up the force. Heavy assault forces should be on hand to deal with large concentrations of insurgents, if necessary. A large, trained civilian political corps must be attached to the effort and work in tandem with designated local leaders to ensure that they assert control over the area and simultaneously restore critical services such as water and electricity.

Denying Access/The Galula Model: Initially the infantry needs to surround the target village, town, small city, or neighborhood. A policing force will then conduct house-to-house searches for insurgents, weapons, and explosives. Once the counterinsurgent forces have saturated the town, authorities can begin a census. Each individual should be recorded, and heads of households should provide any needed family records. The census will provide a baseline for intelligence collection.[3] Biometric data should be collected, and identity cards with encrypted biometric data should be issued to the population. Checkpoints should be established, and ID cards should be checked at random to deter tampering with and counterfeiting the cards. Insurgents will understand the danger this presents to them and strive to discourage the population's compliance.

Sectioning off the population, requiring permission to leave a safe zone for only a limited amount of time, and limiting the

---

[3] David Galula, *Counterinsurgency Warfare: Theory and Practice* (New York: Praeger, 1964).

number of visitors into a particular safe zone by requiring registration and an ID card will significantly reduce violence in the area and provide a considerable measure of security for the population.[4]

Intelligence Collection: Only when the population is completely separated from the bulk of the insurgents and free from intimidation and retribution will volunteers emerge from the population to provide the names of insurgent organizers/recruiters or insurgent support assets still residing among the population. These insurgent recruiters and support assets must be removed from the population so that they cannot repopulate the organization from inside the safe zone. It is important that the loyalty of members of the population be tested. The authorities can test loyalty by sending in intelligence assets (or double agents) posing as insurgents seeking help from among the population. Those who help these double agents should be removed from the safe zone and incarcerated.

Social Organization: Because U.S. democracy relies on its citizens' right to vote freely, Americans considered the Iraqi election in 2005 as a crowning achievement for democracy. The Iraqi voters were brave and faced serious threats in order to exercise their civic duty, but still democracy is not achieved with a single act. The Iraqis must stand up for their rights every day of their lives. In the face of the violence rampant in Iraq, this is a tall request.

To achieve daily support for the participatory government, a political organization among the population is needed in the form of an anti-insurgent patriotic organization. An equivalent of an American Legion, which organizes by block and neighborhood, would be ideal. This social organization would monitor the security of schools, public transportation, etc. It would provide opportunities for all members of the population to vest themselves in a defense against the insurgents. Membership should be rewarded by a government-provided stipend.

Amnesty: As an insurgency loses strength, it would be beneficial to

---

[4] David Galula, *Counterinsurgency Warfare: Theory and Practice* (New York: Praeger, 1964).

offer amnesty to its members for their surrender. As part of an amnesty agreement, insurgents must provide full debriefings on their past activities and up-to-date intelligence on the plans and intentions of active insurgents. Amnesty should include an initial confinement for the purposes of debriefings and time to cross-check and confirm the intelligence provided by the insurgent member who has agreed to lay down arms. Ninety days of confinement is reasonable to accomplish debriefings and confirm information.

The steps of counterinsurgency as noted above are intensive, necessitate significant manpower, and require years to accomplish. Combating insurgents is complicated work, and there is no quick fix. Afghanistan is a multiethnic nation that has been wracked by continuous warfare for almost thirty years. This has produced a generation of individuals who are predominately illiterate, and the members of the educated class either fled or died in nonstop battles. Many of the survivors of the violence can recite the Koran but not read or write in any of their own languages. Seventy percent of the recently recruited and trained police force is illiterate. Thus, the Afghans lack the basic skills needed to conduct a counterinsurgency on their own. Outside forces will need to support Afghanistan in this effort for many years.

Counterinsurgency efforts, as described by David Galula in *Counterinsurgency Warfare: Theory and Practice*, are 10 percent operational and 90 percent political. It is therefore critical that as towns and cities are recovered from insurgent forces, security forces must transfer authority to local civilians, who will drive political reconciliation. The process is long, arduous, and labor intensive.

CRITICAL POINTS

- In counterinsurgency, the population is the key terrain. Until the security of the population is ensured, it will not provide the level of cooperation needed for a counterinsurgency force to route insurgents.

- As soon as key population centers are recaptured, local citizens must be given a stake in governance.

10. ENEMY COMBATANTS
AND INTERROGATION

Following the attacks on September 11, 2001, the U.S. invasion of Afghanistan, the removal of the Taliban, and the destruction of a significant number of al Qaeda's forces, the United States and its allies found themselves with large numbers of enemy combatants—Islamic jihadists fighting under the banner of al Qaeda—populating their prisons. These individuals had gone to Afghanistan either to receive terrorist training or to wage a jihad against the soon to arrive U.S. forces. Jihadists from the Afghan conflict as well as those who have deployed to Iraq represent a minority in the wider Islamic world. They believe that murdering American civilians, U.S. forces, or anyone allied with the United States will advance the interests of the new Islamic order. They do not respect or follow international conventions in regard to the treatment of prisoners. Anyone who falls under their control, including aid workers, journalists, and other noncombatants, is abused, tortured, and murdered.

GUANTANAMO
On June 12, 2008, the U.S. Supreme Court in Boumediene v. Bush decided in a five to four decision that the constitutional right of habeas corpus review (the right to be brought before a judge) applies to persons held in Guantanamo and to persons designated as enemy combatants on that territory. The decision also called the Combatant Status Review Tribunals inadequate. This Supreme Court decision was a blow to current Bush administration policy.

In dissent, Justice Anton Scalia noted, "The Court's majority analysis produces a crazy result. Whereas those convicted and

67

sentenced to death for war crimes are without judicial remedy, all enemy combatants detained during a war, at least insofar as they are confined in an area away from the battlefield over which the United States exercises absolute and indefinite control may seek a writ of habeas corpus."

This decision gives individuals detained for acting as enemy combatants and violating Geneva Conventions standards the legal right of habeas corpus in U.S. courts. It will result in a large number of legal challenges to the detention of those at Guantanamo. Justice Scalia further noted, "Terrorist acts by former prisoners at Guantanamo Bay after their release illustrates the incredible difficulty of assessing who is and who is not an enemy combatant in a foreign theater of operations where the environment does not lend itself to rigorous evidence collection."

A review of the Geneva Conventions is instructive. The Geneva Conventions demand that individuals act in accordance with the established laws of war. Article III of the Geneva Conventions specifically prohibits cruel treatment, torture, and the taking of hostages. How many Westerners have been kidnapped by jihadists groups in Iraq? How many have been beheaded on camera? In Afghanistan, the Taliban committed the rape and murder of Western journalists. The Taliban was also responsible for acts of genocide against ethnic minorities such as the Hazara and Uzbek tribes in northern Afghanistan.

Article Four of the Geneva Conventions gives protections to guerrillas, but only those who meet certain requirements: "(a) that of being commanded by a person responsible for his subordinates; (b) that of having a fixed distinctive sign recognizable at a distance; (c) that of carrying arms openly; (d) that of conducting their operations in accordance with the laws and customs of war." A terrorist who blows up schoolchildren as they receive candy from U.S. troops is not operating in accordance with the laws and customs of war. Neither is a terrorist who uses human shields or operates from a mosque.

Terrorists who do not meet the requirements of the Geneva Conventions are not entitled to its protections and can be executed as marauders or bandits. Few, if any, of the internees at Guantanamo Bay meet the four requirements listed above.

Second, it must be understood that the Guantanamo detainees, shackled, caged, and living behind razor wire, are the most dangerous men on the planet. They shared training in the terrorist camps of Afghanistan, and they received experience in combat against U.S. forces. They are most dangerous because they have had contact with one another within the GITMO prison system, which has allowed them to establish networks within the prison population. If these detainees are freed, they are likely to constitute a deadly international terrorist organization that may surpass al Qaeda in organization and effectiveness.

A short lesson in history is in order. In early 1987 Sheikh Ahmad Yasin of the Gaza Strips' wing of the Muslim Brotherhood formed the Islamic Resistance Movement, which came to be known as Hamas. In December 1992, when confronted with an intifada on the Gaza Strip and the West Bank, Israel rounded up the four hundred Palestinians who were leading the violence against the Jewish state in those territories. The Israelis expelled the organizers across the border into Lebanon. The exiled Palestinians took up residence in a tent city, refused to accept the expulsion, and demanded their return to the occupied territories. They had regular contact with Hezbollah, the deadly Iranian-supported Shia organization known for bombing attacks and years of conflict against Israel. On an almost daily basis, the international media broadcasted images of the Palestinians, living in tents huddled against the cold, and reported on their suffering and isolation. In February 1993, faced with United Nations sanctions and pressure from the Clinton administration, Israeli prime minister Yitzhak Rabin allowed 183 of those expelled to return to the Gaza Strip; the remaining two hundred-plus were allowed to return a year later.

During that period of exile Hamas evolved as a terrorist organization. Those exiled had previously lived in different territories and had not known one another. They used the time together to establish bonds and plan strategies with Hezbollah members. They created an organization more lethal and uncompromising than any other Palestinian terrorist organization.

Hamas conducted its first suicide attack on Israel on April 16, 1993, and expanded its capability exponentially thereafter. Between November 2000 and April 2004 Hamas conducted 425 attacks against Israel, many of them suicide bombings, killing 377 persons and injuring 2,076 persons. At least a dozen American citizens were killed in those attacks.

Returning to the issue of Guantanamo, one must understand that the Bush administration, in an attempt to treat suspects fairly, has already set free a number of prisoners from Guantanamo. At least a dozen have been recaptured or killed on the battlefield since their release. The terrorists who were released from Guantanamo were those who said they were in Afghanistan before their incarceration as businessmen or aid workers; they had been captured as innocent victims fleeing the U.S. invasion. Independent evidence to confirm that these men were members of al Qaeda was lacking. The overwhelming majority of those still held in GITMO were captured as part of armed groups fleeing Afghanistan and have been confirmed as terrorists by foreign governments.

U.S. law prohibits the return of individuals to their home countries, when it is believed that the individuals will be tortured on their return. Since the vast majority of countries in the Middle East torture terrorist suspects or will not accept their return, the United States is stuck with them. The majority of the prisoners held at Guantanamo have received terrorist training from al Qaeda and/or were captured in jihadist elements fighting against the United States. Those who were and will be released will likely build new terrorist organizations with the purpose of striking the United States with, at a minimum, the same level of daring and commitment exhibited by the nineteen September 11 hijackers.

A president must approach enemy combatants from numerous perspectives. How should the law be applied to these jihadists? How can we block jihadists from using their period of incarceration to form groups for the future? And finally, how should the United States address the public relations disaster that followed the Abu Ghraib incidents, in which U.S. military prison guards mistreated Arab prisoners and photographed the acts? On considering these questions, I believe we should close GITMO as quickly as possible and simultaneously try every inmate designated as an enemy combatant. In these trials we should seek the maximum penalty: death.

Most Americans know little about the Guantanamo detainees, their stories, and the extent to which the United States has attempted to apply justice in their circumstances. The case of Mourad Benchellali is instructive. Benchellali, who wrote an op-ed piece about his incarceration in the *New York Times* in 2006, traveled to

Afghanistan on the recommendation of his brother in the summer of 2001 on what he called "a dream vacation." Afghanistan at the time was a place where women were driven around stadiums in the back of pickup trucks on their knees and led off the trucks on leashes to be shot in the back of the head in front of thousands of cheering men. On his arrival in Afghanistan Benchellali found himself in an al Qaeda camp, where he stayed for two months of terrorist training. He claims he could not escape the camp. He also claims that he and others had been lured to Afghanistan by a misguided and mistimed sense of adventure. Shortly after the 9/11 attacks and completion of his training, he and others crossed into Pakistan. Benchellali writes that he was "simply trying to make his way home." Shortly after he crossed into Pakistan, he was taken into custody by the Pakistani army, delivered to the U.S. Army, and named an enemy combatant. He writes, "I was no one's enemy and had never been on a battlefield, let alone aimed a weapon at anyone." After three years at Guantanamo, Benchellali was released to France in 2004 to face charges of having attended terrorism training.

Had Benchellali not been captured in Pakistan and eventually made his way back to France, he likely would have become a terrorist support asset, cell member, or cell leader. Terrorist groups keep track of those they train and call on them for their services. Most terrorists are nervous and afraid when they initially join a group or attend a camp. Gradually, they are brought along and developed into operatives who present a terrible danger to the populations that they live among. Benchellali's claim that he never pointed a gun at anyone means nothing. Those who hijacked the commercial airliners on September 11, 2001, had not used a weapon against anyone until the moment they unleashed their deadly plan, and these men attended the same type of training as Benchellali.

We can only hope that the French will sentence Benchellali to a long period of incarceration. Eventually he and others like him will be free, and our citizens will be seated next to him and others like him on commercial airliners, trains, boats, and buses when traveling the world.

Public support is needed for both continued incarceration and for justice consistent with the detainees' status as enemy combatants. An effort to determine enemy combatants status should be accomplished without further delay.

STANDARDS OF INTERROGATIONS AND PRISONERS' RIGHTS

During the Cold War the United States and the Soviet Union, with their competing ideologies, struggled to determine the future of humankind. The United States and its allies extolled an ideology comprised of representative government, the guarantee of personal freedoms, and an open and competitive economic system. The Soviet Union and its communist allies called for state ownership of property, the subjugation of personal freedom to the demands of the majority, and a centralized owned and directed economy. Both sides possessed nuclear weapons with the capacity to destroy a large portion of the world's population and industrial capacity. Both sides settled into an uneasy status quo and a nuclear policy of mutually assured destruction. Both sides held their forces in abeyance and fought their ideological struggle through surrogates in small wars around the world. Eventually, Soviet ideology could no longer afford the price of suppressing the hundreds of millions of people who were imprisoned under its system.

The United States and its allies now find themselves in yet another struggle. This struggle is far more complex and pits the United States and its allies against nonstate actors, terrorists who, under the mantle of divine direction, employ horrific violence as a means of achieving their policy aims. Jihadists, in the form of Osama bin Laden and al Qaeda, in addition to having conducted the catastrophic attacks of September 11, 2001, have stated their intention to use weapons of mass destruction against the United States and its allies. They have also been able to obtain the religious concurrence (a *fatwa*) of an Islamic authority approving the use of a nuclear device to kill 10 million Americans. When individuals and small groups claim that their intention is to conduct mass murder, the world must pay attention and act aggressively to defend itself. The only restraint on jihadist terrorists is created by the impediments that we construct to delay their acquisition of materials, construction, and delivery of weapons to cause death on a massive scale. With this as a basis for the reality we face, we now can approach a discussion on interrogation.

As part of the response to the attacks on September 11, 2001, the United States has employed harsh interrogation methods against terrorists who have been captured on the battlefield and classified as enemy combatants. Principal members of al Qaeda, who participated in the planning and execution of major terrorist operations and were captured outside Afghanistan and taken into custody by the United States, have been subjected to harsh treatment. The urgent challenge for America is finding a way to live up to the values of human rights and dignity that represent the American ideal. The United States is a signatory to treaties such as the Geneva Conventions and the Convention against Torture; at the same time it must defend itself against terrorists committed to conducting a holocaust against it.

In 2006 President George W. Bush signed the Military Commissions Act, which provided the president with the authority to establish military commissions to try terrorists and unlawful enemy combatants. With the signing of the Military Commissions Act, strict guidelines for interrogations by U.S. military personnel were established. A new U.S. Army field manual, *2-22.3 Human Intelligence Collector Operations*, defines the new parameters of interrogation. Without divulging specific weaknesses, I can say that these new tactics and approaches have a number of faults to the extent that I would say that those captured on the battlefield are treated with greater care than are U.S. citizens taken into custody in the United States. The new field manual makes the interrogator's job almost impossible. Though we must ensure that prisoners' rights are respected, we still have a responsibility to question individuals captured on the battlefield, with weapons and improvised explosives on their bodies and intelligence of impending attacks in their heads. An honest review of the new 2006 policy and its effects is in order.

The CIA's ability to interrogate terrorists is not addressed in the Military Commissions Act and neither is how the United States should handle terrorists who are captured and found to be involved in the production, sale, or use of weapons of mass destruction (WMD). Should the CIA or FBI capture a terrorist found to possess traces of weapons-grade plutonium or vials of weaponized biological materials, a president will find him or herself in new territory. Should the arresting officers read such suspects their Miranda rights and introduce them to a lawyer?

Because of the destruction they could wreak on the country, individuals captured and/or linked to weapons of mass destruction should be considered as a separate category under the law. The United States must explore the possibility of putting in place some extraordinary measures, possibly the use of pharmaceuticals, to deal with a WMD suspect. This recommendation is controversial and may seem contrary to basic principles of American justice. However, today, it takes only a small group of individuals to murder millions and present a threat to the nation's existence. Following the attacks on September 11, 2001, numerous government officials stated that they simply could not imagine such an attack before it happened. That excuse only works once per generation. The phrase first said by Abraham Lincoln and later by Justice Robert H. Jackson must be considered: "The Constitution of the United States and its amendments should not be a suicide pact."

Though torturing another person is terrible to contemplate, because of the nature of the international order and the availability of technology today the U.S. government would be wise to discuss other options more fully. Al Qaeda is not the only group in recent history that has planned to employ weapons of mass destruction. The Japanese group Aum Shinrikyo harnessed the power of hundreds of highly educated individuals to develop WMDs in a twisted plan to cause a global catastrophe so that their leader Ashahara could ascend to world power. The group launched Sarin attacks in the Tokyo subway system, but Japanese authorities were able to arrest their leader and dismantle the group's incredibly potent and growing WMD capability before it was used to kill millions.

CRITICAL POINTS

- Close GITMO as quickly as possible and establish a mechanism to legally attach enemy combatant status to those detainees where evidence exists to confirm such status.

- Enemy combatants are not eligible for the full protection under the Geneva Conventions. When enemy combatants are captured they should be given an option: cooperate in debriefings or face a judicial system that will aim to have them executed if found guilty.

- Establish a protocol for the handling of any individual captured with material that indicates a strong likelihood of an imminent WMD attack.

- Conduct an examination of the effectiveness of interro-

gations conducted by military personnel of captured insurgents employing the new guidelines.

11. COUNTERTERRORISM:

POLICY

The United States and its allies are locked in a battle against terrorists and jihadists who desire to impose a new order over much of the world. They believe that violent terrorist acts are the most effective means of both achieving international publicity and applying pressure to the American electorate to meet their demands.

The United States policy on terrorism states, "The United States will make no concessions to terrorists." The statement is strong. The statement is unequivocal and presents in clear terms that we will not negotiate. However, I recommend a slight alteration of this policy.

Terrorists who hold hostages or threaten barbaric action against innocents have multiple aims. Not only are they seeking publicity and influence over U.S. policy, but most important, they are attempting to humiliate and discredit our national leadership. Even if the United States achieves all of its Homeland Security goals and completely denies terrorists the ability to enter and organize inside the country, Americans who travel in great numbers or work abroad will still be vulnerable. A hostage situation whether at home or abroad will present a president with difficult choices.

Let us consider the following: a planeload of hostages is being held and the terrorists holding them are willing to release half of the hostages in return for food and water. This exchange would be favorable and simultaneously further our goal of reducing the number of hostages being held. So, in this case, the U.S. government would negotiate the exchange, notwithstanding its stated no concession policy.

Unfortunately, given the nature of the world, a terrorist group could position itself to conduct a horrific act with such terrible consequences that a president may be forced to release prisoners or compelled to make some other concession benefiting the terrorists. Even Israel, a country that is tough on terrorism, has been forced into prisoner trades. In this circumstance the president must ensure that no action the United States takes is irreversible.[1]

Considering these examples, it becomes clear that the United States would be better served to have a policy that reads, "The United States will make no meaningful concessions to terrorists." The operative word here is *meaningful.* One must realize that if a circumstance compels a president to take some action, such as releasing an individual from incarceration, that act should be reversible. (In the example of releasing a criminal from prison, the act is reversible in that the criminal can be recaptured.) Also, one must bear in mind that no country is obligated to follow through on any agreement made as a result of extortion. The moment a government recovers hostages, it is free to respond with lethal attacks against those who threatened our interests.

It is critical to understand that I do not favor concessions to terrorists. I favor providing U.S. leadership with freedom of movement and the flexibility to avoid being discredited or embarrassed as a result of a terrorist situation. I support strengthening the hands of the president, not needlessly binding them.[2]

I recommend no immediate announcement of a change in policy. If a president finds him or herself in difficult circumstances, he or she can simply announce the adjustment provided here: "The United States will make no meaningful concessions to terrorists." And this step should be taken only when wiggle room is needed.

CRITICAL POINTS

- Terrorists aim to discredit our national leadership.
- All those involved in counterterrorism must know and understand the government's policy on counterterrorism.

---

[1] Paul Pillar, *Terrorism and U.S. Foreign Policy* (Washington, DC: Brookings Institution Press, 2001).

[2] Ibid.

- The government's counterterrorism policy must provide space and flexibility.
- We are under no obligation to follow through on any agreement secured under duress.

12. WEAPONS OF MASS DESTRUCTION

Apresident and his or her staff will receive numerous briefings on weapons of mass destruction on entering office. These briefings will address threats of a nuclear, chemical, biological, and radiological nature. The president must formulate responses to these potential threats with consideration of the facts in terms of difficulty of execution for terrorist groups, and he or she must also assess the effectiveness of preventative measures currently undertaken.

NUCLEAR TERRORISM

The first threat relative to nuclear terrorism consists of potential theft of a weapon from the arsenal of one of the nations that possess nuclear weapons. The second nuclear threat is the potential fabrication of an improvised nuclear weapon by a terrorist group. Third is the possibility that a government might willingly turn a weapon over to a terrorist group. And finally there is the potential that political instability may cause a government to lose control of a nuclear weapon. Michael Levi does an outstanding job of addressing these specific threats in his book *On Nuclear Terrorism.*

The centerpiece of U.S. nonproliferation efforts is the Nunn-Lugar Act, the Cooperative Threat Reduction Program. This program was conceived and championed by former Senator Sam Nunn of Georgia and currently serving Senator Richard Lugar of Indiana. The Nunn-Lugar Act took great steps to reduce the availability of nuclear weapons and material terrorists might attempt to acquire. The act was signed into law in 1991 and allowed for joint destruction of nuclear weapons exceeding the drawdown thresholds the United States and Soviet Union had previously agreed to. It simultaneously upgraded the security of existing stockpiles to defend against outside theft and threat of inside weapons and material diversion. The program also included an effort to help former nuclear scientists and weapons engineers in the former Soviet Union find employment outside the nuclear weapons field. Providing such incentives deterred the sale of lethal knowledge on the black market.[1]

In 2002 the G-8 initiated a program in concert with the United States to complement the Nunn-Lugar Act, referred to as the Global Partnership. Under the Global Partnership, the G-8 and the United States each committed to spend 10 billion dollars over the next decade to further enhance the security of nuclear weapons and materials stocks. The enhanced security consists of a broad system of material and technology controls and an internal accounting of fissile material, enriched uranium, and plutonium needed to achieve a nuclear yield.

The act allowed for the dismantlement and destruction of over five thousand nuclear warheads in the United States and former Soviet Union for pennies on the dollar. This nonpartisan effort began a new era. If there were ever two individuals in America who deserve the Presidential Medal of Freedom, they are Sam Nunn and Richard Lugar for their extraordinary contribution to world security.

More than twenty years ago I watched a *60 Minutes* news segment in which the interviewer sat in the kitchen of an average American home and assembled a mock improvised nuclear weapon. The image of this bowling ball–sized fissile material encased in a large metal saucer on a kitchen table implied the process was as simple as using the Easy-Bake Oven. While this demonstration made great theater, it was hardly accurate. After watching the segment Americans could all imagine some disgruntled housewife assembling this device after sending the kids off to school and wiping out a congressional district from the comfort of her own kitchen.

If it really were so easy, then countries with billions of petrodollars and thousands of scientists and engineers, like Iraq under Saddam Hussein, Iran under the Mullahs, and Libya under Kaddafi, would not have so far failed in their concealed efforts to build such

---

[1] Michael Levi, *On Nuclear Terrorism* (Cambridge: Harvard University Press, 2007).

a weapon. The truth is the engineering needed to fabricate such a device is incredibly complex and currently beyond a terrorist group's capabilities. The CIA's efforts to identify and track the illegal proliferation activities of A. Q. Khan, the father of the Pakistani nuclear programs, was incredibly important in containing this threat. What is important to recognize is that significant efforts by U.S. political leaders on both sides of the aisle have contributed greatly to keeping nuclear weapons and material out of terrorist groups' hands, and we need to support continued innovation to block terrorists from obtaining such a weapon.

The only threat the Nunn-Lugar Act doesn't protect us against is the potential collapse of a nuclear state. The United States, Russia, China, the United Kingdom, France, Israel, India, Pakistan, and North Korea currently possess nuclear weapons. Of these, Pakistan and North Korea are particularly dangerous because either of their governments could collapse from political or economic instability, leaving their nuclear arsenals up for grabs.[2] The loss of these weapons and their firing codes would present a terrible threat to world security, and only the United States has the capability and international power to intervene and influence the outcome in such a difficult and complex situation. It is therefore critical that the U.S. commander in chief possess mastery over the national security apparatus. To lack this knowledge places the United States and the world at risk.

CHEMICAL WEAPONS

The threat posed by chemical weapons is more difficult to guard against than that posed by nuclear weapons. The Aum Shinrikyo's 1995 sarin attacks in Tokyo's subway system illustrate how a group might employ chemical weapons. For these attacks, Aum Shinrikyo planted airtight containers filled with liquid sarin on five subway cars following three different tracks that converged underground near several government ministries. The group punctured the containers with umbrellas and left them to leak the liquid sarin, which slowly evaporated into a lethal gas. The attack killed twelve people and left 5,700 injured. This example shows how dual-use technolo-

---

[2] Michael Levi, *On Nuclear Terrorism* (Cambridge: Harvard University Press, 2007).

gies, or technologies that can be used for both peaceful and military aims, can easily be exploited by small criminal or terrorist organizations.

Industrial chemical plant sabotage by terrorist groups is another potential threat in this category. In the 1984 disaster in Bhopal, India, for example, forty tons of methyl isocyanate (MIC) gas were released into the atmosphere at Bhopal's Union Carbide subsidiary pesticide plant. The gas killed approximately 3,800 people immediately, and it is estimated that twenty thousand people have died prematurely since the incident. About 200,000 people were injured.

If so many deaths can occur in a chemical plant *accident*, what would a planned attack against a facility close to a U.S. city look like? To defend against this scenario, the U.S. government must establish layered defenses. These defenses include a substantial investment in the physical security of chemical installations. An installation's employees must be screened, and we must make a national commitment to fund, train, and deploy sufficient counterterrorism (CT) personnel. Trained and ready local, state, and federal law enforcement CT personnel are necessary to identify, penetrate, and disrupt activities before they occur.

BIOLOGICAL WEAPONS

The biological threat is the single greatest threat to U.S. national security and well-being. Nuclear and chemical attacks, though devastating, can be contained and responded to in kind. A biological attack, however, presents a completely different array of difficulties. Biological agents used in an attack can spread through contact from one person to another across the country, and this spread may not be recognized until the first affected patients begin to seek medical attention. By the time patients seek a doctor's help, they'll have already passed the disease to others. Hundreds, thousands, even millions could die from such an attack, especially if the biological agent is significantly virulent and medical personnel have trouble identifying and then countering it. A biological attack using Marburg, the Ebola group, smallpox, plague, or any of another half dozen agents, with genetic alterations to resist antibi-

---

[3] Ken Alibek, *Biohazard: The Chilling True Story of the Largest Covert Biological Weapons Program in the World—Told from the Inside by the Man Who Ran It*, with Stephen Handelman (New York: Random House, 1999).

otics, would present a serious threat to Americans' survival as a people.[3] An attack would change living and working arrangements and essentially alter the social contract among Americans. Travel of a biological agent beyond U.S. borders and to the developing world, where medical facilities and government resources are limited, would present an even greater threat.

In the 1980s the former Soviet Union, in violation of international agreements, conducted advanced study on creating antibiotic-resistant strains of several of the most dangerous diseases.[4] Had one of these genetically engineered bioweapons been released premeditatedly on the United States or accidentally in the former Soviet Union, the world would be a very different and frightening place today.

Planning the government response to the release of a bioweapon should be the highest national priority in terms of weapons of mass destruction. A new president must immediately propose legislation strengthening our national medical system. This legislation should include supporting increased local stockpiles of appropriate supplies and government financial support. Support should provide wider availability of medical facilities, including reverse pressure rooms to treat victims and contain the potential spread of a biologic agent through the population. The U.S. government should subsidize specifically targeted upgrades of medical capability for use in a national emergency. Both standing capability and significant deployable mobile resources must be developed immediately. A national quarantine plan should be established, and citizens must be made aware of the stark reality of an infectious disease's burnout cycle.

The current approach to biological threat is to stockpile vaccines. Dr. Ken Alibek, who served in the Soviet bioweapons program before defecting to the United States, noted that the variety of potential bioweapons makes a vaccine route of defenses ineffective. Alibek is pursuing the development of different medical approaches to face these threats. What is needed now is a bipartisan approach to chart and fund a program to enhance U.S. defenses against biological attack.

RADIOLOGICAL WEAPONS

[4] Ken Alibek, *Biohazard: The Chilling True Story of the Largest Covert Biological Weapons Program in the World—Told from the Inside by the Man Who Ran It,* with Stephen Handelman (New York: Random House, 1999).

A radiological weapon is frequently called a dirty bomb. In radiological attacks explosives in combination with toxic material are dispersed over an area, making it uninhabitable. Radiological attack is the simplest and least destructive of WMD methodologies. This kind of attack is most destructive if it occurs in an important government or commercial area. Given the low level of technical expertise needed to combat a radiological attack, the U.S. government need only require a continued effort in basic levels of intelligence and security and develop technologies to aide in decontamination of potentially affected areas.

CRITICAL POINTS

- The Nunn-Lugar Act and the Joint G-8-U.S. Global Partnership have provided the basis for reduction, control, and destruction of nuclear weapons and material. This legislation should be the model for all counterproliferation efforts.

- Though it is unlikely that a terrorist group will steal or fabricate a nuclear weapon, the potential for loss of a weapon in a collapsing Pakistan or North Korea will require the highest level of presidential leadership and sound decision-making. Prepare for the eventuality now.

- Biological weapons present a threat to U.S. existence and require a bipartisan plan to rapidly address current shortfalls in preparation for such a situation.

13. CATASTROPHIC EVENT RESPONSE

As the world's preeminent political and military power, the United States will continue to be the target of aggrieved groups. Hope for the best but plan for the worst is a sound way to approach this possibility of catastrophic terrorism. In addition to the weapons of mass destruction discussed in chapter 12, terrorists can employ conventional technology and modern industrial processes to cause widespread death and destruction. The level of commitment in terms of resources, manpower, and focus that will be required should the United States experience such a catastrophic terrorist attack is immense.

PREPARATION FOR IMMEDIATE RESPONSE

The most significant problem the United States has in terms of responding to a national or regional disaster is dealing with its large population centers. The United States consists of dozens of major cities and urban areas with populations in excess of 10 million people. Evacuation from these areas is the first and most critical problem of disaster management and preparation. Houston, a city of 2.5 million people, did a remarkable job of evacuating its populace in 2005, before Hurricane Rita. The city government moved up to 90 percent of its population before the hurricane hit. The evacuation took several days, and citizens, mindful of the collective city, state, and federal failures in the aftermath of Hurricane Katrina, which had hit the Gulf Coast a month earlier, were eager to comply with the city government's orders.

It is important to understand that during a catastrophic terrorist attack the government may order an evacuation without giving the populace advanced warning. A large portion of the infrastructure may be destroyed, making communication of this order difficult. The population will panic when communication systems go offline, mass transit stops functioning, and major roads close. Many families may become separated.

The U.S. Federal Emergency Management Agency (FEMA) works with city and state governments to facilitate a response to regional and national disasters and provides aid to victims. FEMA's approach of allowing state and local governments to draft and manage their own emergency plans makes good sense. Local officials understand the needs of the local population better than the federal government does. However, when state and local governments are overwhelmed by a crisis, FEMA and the federal government must assert themselves much more firmly.

In events that involve the death or injury of tens of thousands of people, the Department of Defense will be required to provide logistic, rescue, and security support to relieve the suffering of the city that has been attacked. The military is prepared to respond to such emergencies, but its deployments in Iraq and Afghanistan make expanding its current domestic response role difficult.

Frequently the Posse Comitatus Act of 1878 is referenced when decision-makers discuss military participation in domestic activities. This act makes it criminal for the military to participate in law enforcement unless expressly authorized by the Constitution or the Congress. The passage of the Posse Comitatus Act was part of a post–Civil War compromise with the Southern states and facilitated the removal of federal troops from the South. In the case of disaster relief, the act allows troops to enter a state in response to a crisis if they remain in action subordinate to civilian authorities.

Although the U.S. military is stretched thin with overseas deployments, a division of reservists or a significant portion of the National Guard should expand their training and be equipped to participate and support response to catastrophic events. This training should include becoming familiar with emergency rescue, triage, first aid, and heavy equipment operation. This mission is different from the soldiers' traditional combat role, but the military's small unit leadership, discipline, and teamwork will provide successful support to this type of mission. The National Guard from several states as far a way as Oregon responded immediately to

Hurricane Katrina, but not all of these guard units had been trained to respond to large-scale disasters. Meanwhile the Coast Guard was well prepared for the emergency, and its performance in rescue operations during Hurricane Katrina saved thousands of lives and highlights the military's significant abilities and potential in crisis. In the event of a nuclear, chemical, or biological attack, the military's support would be critical to ensure the U.S. government would be able to successfully execute its national response plan.

PREPARATION OF MEDICAL RESPONSE

A significant number of people were killed during the September 11, 2001, attacks and Hurricane Katrina in 2005; however, neither of these events overwhelmed America's medical system. Had the United States suffered losses equivalent to the 2004 Boxing Day Tsunami, which killed more than 225,000 people, or the 1976 Tangshan, China, earthquake, in which 240,000 died and 200,000 were injured, its medical system would have been overwhelmed. Those two large events need to be the models the government uses when considering the difficulties its citizenry will encounter following a catastrophic terrorist attack.

The United States has made progress in training first responders in its major cities and has provided decontamination capability where needed. Should there be a significant terrorist attack, it is certain America will rebuild. It cannot, however, replace lost lives and therefore needs a medical system that can save as many people as possible.

The U.S. government maintains under the Health and Human Services Department a National Disaster Medical System (NDMS). The NDMS maintains a roster of nine thousand medical responders across the country. Teams of these responders will deploy to the crisis area to deliver medical services, to care for the injured, and to prepare the injured when possible for medivac to a facility outside the affected area for longer-term care. It takes several days, however, to move the responders to the crisis site and deliver and set up the necessary equipment. Blocked roads, contaminated areas, and fires, for example, can slow entry into areas affected by a disaster.

In the event of a biological attack, negative pressure rooms are required to decrease the risk of spreading biological agents. These rooms are expensive and in short supply. Basic medical supplies are similarly scarce. Costs make it difficult for hospitals to purchase and maintain supplies. Thus, hospitals do not keep extra supplies in stock, preferring instead to buy them as they need them. Federal and state governments should create incentives for the hospitals to increase capability, especially when it comes to building negative pressure rooms and stocking basic supplies.

In many types of disasters, the greatest number of injuries occurs immediately. Once their injuries are healed, the patients are released and, within a few days or weeks, the number of patients in a hospitals' care is diminished. In a biological, nuclear, or radiological attack, time will produce more patients as a biological agent is passed to more victims or as toxins spread through communities.

VOLUNTEER SUPPORT

Should a catastrophic terrorist attack occur, rescue forces will deploy immediately, but realistically, it will take several days for sufficient forces to reach the site and begin to mitigate the suffering. Thus it will be necessary for all Americans to step up and participate in the national effort. No government in the world can adequately respond to a catastrophic terrorist attack without the help of thousands of organized volunteers who are willing to work to save their fellow citizens. In World War II, for example, a British expeditionary force was trapped on the beaches of Dunkirk while the Nazis prepared to destroy them. All appeared lost for England's young men until on the horizon appeared thousands of private vessels. A joint effort by government and private citizens launched this fleet, which sailed into air attacks and artillery fire to save their army. Thousands of men were taken off the beaches before the Nazis could destroy the British force.

One cannot underestimate the importance of having a president front and center explaining the dimensions of a catastrophe early on. Americans understand that massive destruction impedes rescue and will give a president the time to act, but even as the president works to coordinate and deploy aid, he or she must communicate the facts of the crisis and exhibit leadership to the people. Americans who volunteer at the risk to their own lives to save fellow citizens will need to be directed in an organized fashion.

CRITICAL POINTS

- When considering preparation for catastrophic events, use the known worst-case scenarios for modeling.

- The quality of our medical and logistic responses will directly affect who lives and who dies.

- The challenges of consequence management following a WMD attack or huge natural disaster are likely to outstrip state and federal resources. A president and staff needs to be prepared to direct large, self-initiating private rescue efforts by Americans in addition to the federal effort.

14. IRAN, THE KEY STATE SPONSOR OF TERRORISM

As of 2008, Iran continues to play the role of political spoiler in the Middle East and is the principal state sponsor of terrorism in the world. The average American knows little about Iranian history or the details of the U.S. relationship with Iran over the past fifty years. A large number of Iranians, however, have detailed knowledge of the history of this relationship, and this knowledge constitutes the prism through which they view the world. It is important to understand that the Iranian population is intensely proud of its Persian heritage, which spans back two thousand years and was the birthplace of science, culture, art, and an impressive line of warriors.

The United States became involved in Iran in earnest following the conclusion of World War II, as Britain began a withdrawal of its commitments in the Middle East. During the Cold War, the United States intervened in Iranian internal political affairs in order to remove Iran's popularly elected prime minister, Mohammad Mosaddeq, and reinstall the Pahlavi Dynasty by putting Mohammad Reza Shah Pahlavi on the Iranian throne. This effort was spearheaded by CIA officer Kermit Roosevelt and recounted in his book *Countercoup*. The coup advanced U.S. and British commercial interests and initiated Iran's rapid program of economic, social, and military development.

In the early 1960s President John F. Kennedy pressured Reza Shah Pahlavi to quicken the pace of social reform in his country. This brought on the Shah's White Revolution, whereby women received expanded rights and opportunities. The White Revolution engendered the opposition of Iran's Shia clergy, which was led by a relatively young Ayatollah Khomeini. Khomeini was eventually expelled, organized abroad for two decades, and returned to lead the Shah's overthrow and creation of a Shia theocracy in 1979.

Americans love to talk about the genius of the creators of the U.S. Constitution. Separate branches of government and a system of checks and balances have allowed the American political experiment to thrive for more than 225 years. The Iranians, in the creation of their theocracy, created similar checks and balances. Iranians have a democratic system, but that system is established to ensure the continuation of the theocratic regime. In effect, the system allows Islamic fundamentalists to dominate the Iranian political landscape and retain power. In the past, purported reformers have been elected to high office, and the international community has held the false belief that these reformers would somehow transform the Iranian political system. This has not occurred because Islamic theocrats ensure final power in the Iranian system through legal and religious review.

The members of Iran's Assembly of Experts, a group of mullahs, are elected by the populace. The assembly in turn chooses a supreme leader (*faqih*). The supreme leader is the most important Islamic authority and the head of state. He must be a member of the Shia clergy and a noted Islamic scholar. The supreme leader commands the armed forces and is the only one in the Iranian government who can declare war.

The Council of Guardians is the most powerful institution in the Iranian government. Six of its twelve members are chosen by the supreme leader. These members are Shia clergy. The other six are chosen by the judiciary, and while they may not be clergy, they must be Islamic scholars. The Council of Guardians approves presidential candidates and examines and approves candidates who wish to run for the Iranian parliament (the Majles). The Council of Guardians reviews laws to ensure compliance with the constitution and Shari'ah law. Though Iran has a president and a parliament, it is easy to see that its system allows the mullahs to contain reform and continue in power.

A parade of wishful-thinking policy experts in Washington have spent the better part of two and a half decades in search of Iranian moderates who would deliver the Iranian people from the murderous policies pursued by the Iranian theocracy. Only with the election of President Mahmoud Ahmadinejad has this Pollyanna chorus finally been silenced. Ahmadinejad has spoken openly of his desire to destroy the State of Israel.

The Iranian theocratic regime learned from its inception that violence, terror, and murder are effective forms of foreign policy. Iran's theocrats used terror in the process of overthrowing the shah. They used terror to eliminate the leftist Mujahedin-e Khalq organization, with which they had cooperated to remove the monarchy, and in the state-sponsored kidnapping, torture, and murder of internal political opponents.

In its dealings with the United States, Iran has supported the creation of terrorist organizations outside Iran and used such organizations, including Lebanese Hezbollah, to conduct attacks on U.S. interests, and the United States has failed to respond to any of these attacks in a meaningful way. After 241 marines were killed in a deadly bombing at the Marine barracks in Beirut, the Reagan administration planned an attack on Lebanese Hezbollah, which had conducted the attack, and Iran in the Bekaa Valley of Lebanon only to have Secretary of Defense Caspar Weinberger cancel the operation at the last minute. The Reagan administration's failure to respond emboldened both Iran and Hezbollah to continue their horrific terrorist actions.

Thirteen years later, in 1996, Iran funded a joint attack by Saudi Hezbollah, known as Hezbollah al-Hijaz, and Lebanese Hezbollah on Khobar Towers in Saudi Arabia, where the U.S. Air Force housed its personnel, aimed at killing four hundred U.S. airmen. The attack was foiled by an alert U.S. Air Force security detachment, which noticed a tanker truck parked near the housing complex perimeter and promptly began an evacuation. Because of the security detachment's efforts only nineteen died in the attack, but more than three hundred of various nationalities were injured.

This Iran-sponsored attack was a clear act of war, but the Clinton administration refused to retaliate. FBI Director Louis Freeh contacted former President George Herbert Walker Bush, who in turn convinced the Saudi government to provide the FBI with access to those captured in Saudi Arabia in connection with the attack. The Clinton White House did not help with Freeh's effort, which ultimately uncovered Iran's role in the attack. Still, even with the evidence that Iran had backed the terrorist organizations involved, the U.S. administration did nothing.

This inaction remains a problem today. The George W. Bush administration has announced repeatedly that Iran is funding, training, and arming those that conduct IED attacks on U.S. forces in Iraq, yet he has failed to act in defense of those under his command. Because of U.S. negligence, Iran has learned that terrorism is an effective form of foreign policy; it will pay no price when murdering U.S. forces and civilians.

Iran's terrorist efforts could force either the United States or Israel to act with military force against Iran. The country is publicly pursuing enriched uranium, an essential element of its nuclear weapons program. The Iranian parliament has voted unanimously that pursuit of enriched uranium is not only the country's right but also the government's responsibility. Iran has used its status as a signatory of the Nuclear Nonproliferation Treaty (NPT) to assemble much of what it needs to achieve a viable nuclear weapons program in the years ahead.[*]

At the same time, the United States must also be prepared for a preemptive Israeli attack on Iran's nuclear facilities. Iran's recent refusal to comply with the International Atomic Energy Commission (IAEA) in regard to its efforts to achieve weapons-grade uranium, its call for the complete destruction of the State of Israel, and its continued arming of Hezbollah for attacks on Israel are destabilizing to the region. Iran's direct support for Hezbollah's attacks on Israel led Israel to enter Lebanon in 2006 in an effort to rescue its kidnapped soldiers, end the firing of rockets at Israeli cities, and repel Hezbollah from key sectors in south Lebanon.

With regard to Iran, the United States has two choices. It can pursue policies that might alter Iranian behavior, or it can pursue policies that will result in regime change. Given the intensity of opposition to the United States and its policies that the Islamic Iranian regime demonstrates on a daily basis, it is unlikely that Iran can be compelled to alter its policies by international sanctions. The United States therefore must face the difficult fact that regime change in Iran is the best long-term course of action. Regime change will not be easy, simple, or without risk. The alternative, however, is that Iran will continue and ultimately succeed in its

---

[*] Jerome R. Corsi, *Atomic Iran: How the Terrorist Regime Bought the Bomb and American Politicians* (Nashville: WND Books, 2005).

desire to contruct nuclear weapons and continue to support violence against Israel.

In the past, the United States has had contact with Iranian oppositionists who themselves desire regime change. Those contacts were never much more than an effort to maintain a window into these oppositionists' activities. The United States should initiate a major effort to replace the Iranian theocratic regime with a government that will cease support of terrorism and end Iranian efforts to construct nuclear weapons. As part of this process, an Iranian government in exile should be created and funded. Such an organization can serve as a rallying point for those opposed to the current regime's activities. The United States recently initiated support of a free Persian news service outside of Iran, called Farda (Tomorrow), that challenges Iranian policies and news reporting on a daily basis, much as Radio Free Europe did during the Cold War. This service should also be used as a means of rallying Iranians to the government in exile.

Because the United States has given Iran a pass on its terrorist activities in the past, the Iranians believe that the United States is weak, overstretched, and afraid to confront them in a meaningful way. This will lead the Iranians to miscalculate as Saddam Hussein did in both 1991 and 2003, when he refused to believe the United States would attack. Further, Iran's failure to abide by UN Security Council resolutions will likely ultimately compel the United States to conduct limited attacks on Iran's nuclear and advanced weapons facilities in order to delay the country's eventual development of a nuclear weapons program. In response, Iran will use terrorists and militias in Iraq to attack both U.S. and coalition forces in locations where it can achieve numerical and military advantages. As tensions heighten, it is critical that U.S. and coalition forces in Iraq are maintained in sufficient mass to defend against Iranian surrogate attacks.

The Iranian Revolutionary Guard Corps (IRGC) is the arm of the Iranian government responsible for repeated attacks on U.S. interests and personnel. The corps is arming special groups in southern Iraq with IED technology such as enhanced formed projectiles (EFPs) so that they may kill and maim U.S. military personnel. The IRGC also conducts small boat operations in the Persian Gulf. Iranian coastal defense forces have Chinese-made C-801/803 antiship missiles and employ shoot-and-scoot tactics, meaning they can fire and then quickly move to another location where they can fire again, and so on. The Iranian navy operates somewhat larger ships than the IRGC and has several Kilo-class submarines; neither would be too difficult to find and sink in the Persian Gulf's shallow waters.

The IRGC navy's tactics fall in line with their asymmetrical approach to warfare, which they have designed to counter superior U.S. firepower and technology. The Iranians will enter an engagement with no expectation of winning an outright military victory against U.S. forces but rather with the goal of swarming and sacrificing hundreds if not a thousand of their men to sink just one major U.S. naval vessel and thereby inflict mass casualties. The Iranian goal in asymmetrical warfare is to deliver high casualties and thereby garner a negative reaction from the U.S. public, which, the Iranians anticipate, would then cause a commander in chief to withdraw from the conflict to limit further casualties.

The Shiites of Iran and Lebanese Hezbollah who have had regular military engagements with the Israeli defense forces since 1982 are defined not by their wins and losses but by their willingness to fight. Dealing with Iran and Hezbollah requires patience, commitment, nerve, and moral clarity. Iran does not possess the size, strength, or international ideological appeal that the Soviet Union had at the height of the Cold War. As Persians and members of the Shiite sect—a minority sect in the Muslim world—their appeal is limited. That said, the Iranian pursuit of nuclear technology as a possible guarantor of the theocratic regime's long-term survival, its role of primary state sponsor of terrorism, and its accompanying threats to the region make for extreme danger.

Should the Iranians attempt any provocative action, such as attempting to seize U.S. personnel—as they did British sailors and marines in April 2007—or firing on U.S. vessels, the United States should take advantage of this opportunity and destroy the dozen or so IRGC naval facilities and all IRGC vessels in the Persian Gulf right away. Should the Iranians make any effort to close the Straits of Hormuz at the mouth of the Persian Gulf, the U.S. attack could include destroying Iranian oil refineries. This would likely put the regime in significant danger, as it would destroy the basis for the entire Iranian economy.

CRITICAL POINTS

- The failure by both Republican and Democratic administrations during the past twenty-eight years to respond to Iranian attacks on U.S. forces and citizens either directly by Iranian intelligence officers and Revolutionary Guards or through terrorist proxies such as Hezbollah, has led the Iranians to the conclusion that the United States is weak, afraid, and unwilling to risk a military engagement. The difficulties that the United States is facing in Iraq only add to this Iranian view. The Iranian regime, believing the United States will not act against it, will likely attack U.S. interests, causing a U.S. response of significant military force.

- In the event of open hostilities between the United States and Iran, Iran will likely use asymmetrical tactics against U.S. forces in Iraq and in the Persian Gulf.

- The United States should sponsor an Iranian government in exile and expand existing programs designed to challenge the legitimacy of the Islamic regime.

- Iran is pursuing nuclear weapons technology to ensure the Islamic regime's survival.

15. THE NEW WAR

While driving a Humvee in July 2003, Specialist Joel Bertoldie was killed in Fallujah, Iraq, by an improvised explosive device (IED). He was the first recorded IED casualty. Since then, the number of IED attacks in Iraq and Afghanistan has increased at an exponential rate. The press has reported that Afghanistan witnessed close to 1,400 IED attacks in 2006 and that 28,000 occurred in Iraq. Over half of all combat casualties in the Iraqi and Afghan theaters of operations are caused by the deadly employment of IEDs.

In response, the United States, with the participation of the United Kingdom, Canada, Australia, and New Zealand, created the Joint Improvised Explosive Device Defeat Organization (JIEDDO). With a headquarters staff of 350 in northern Virginia, JIEDDO is a multinational, multiservice organization staffed with service personnel, scientists, and analysts dedicated to defeating the IED threat. JIEDDO personnel study the variety of technical and operational characters of all types of IEDs, including human bombers, roadside devices, and vehicular-born devices. With this information, they educate soldiers and help them survive attacks. JIEDDO task forces in Iraq and Afghanistan, consisting of a combination of soldiers, sailors, airmen, marines, and civilian experts, augment tactical units with personnel, technology, analysis, and resources to combat IED attacks. The explosives ordinance disposal (EOD) community is critical to JIEDDO's mission. JIEDDO's budget for 2007 was four billion, and for 2008 it is 13 billion dollars. While some in Congress have questioned JIEDDO's performance, had JIEDDO not been created, the United States and its coalition partners would likely have suffered many times more casualties from IEDs.

In the long term, the multiple networks conducting IED attacks on U.S. and coalition forces, many of which consist of non-Iraqis and non-Afghans, present an asymmetrical threat to every country in the Middle East and South Asia. Because of lax border controls and the illegal sale of official documents, these IED cells, like the Arab-Afghan fighters of the Soviet jihad period, are likely to carry their trade with them out of these battlefields and into bordering nations.

The U.S. military currently conducts the process of identifying and linking terrorist IED networks, which involves identifying specific cell leaders, IED makers/engineers, and teams of emplacers (the people who put the IEDs in the ground). While the military carries out this duty competently, the information it uncovers must be made easily accessible to U.S. civilian intelligence and law enforcement agencies. Today's IED cell members and leaders will likely be the major terrorist leaders of the next decades. Thus, it is critical in the IED fight to ensure that everyone involved understands that this is a fight not only against IED devices but also against the networks that fund, create, and plant such deadly instruments.

The most deadly of IEDs is known as the explosively formed projectile (EFP). An EFP's design and material allows it to penetrate most U.S. armor, and this, of course, results in high U.S. and coalition force casualties in IED attacks made with EFPs. These EFPs have been traced back to a source in Iran, the number-one state sponsor of terrorism (see chapter 14). In early April 2008, components sufficient to assemble a thousand EFPs were recovered in one cache in southern Iraq, and it has been discovered that Iran was the originator of these materials.

CRITICAL POINTS

- JIEDDO must be well funded and receive broad support in order to continue to conduct its important mission.

- JIEDDO must expand it efforts from those against "the device" to more broad efforts to identify and destroy IED networks in order to slow the movement of the networks out of the Iraq and Afghan theaters into neighboring countries.

16. PARAMILITARY AND SPECIAL OPERATIONS CAPABILITY

Over the last decade numerous debates about how to improve paramilitary and special operations capability have occurred among U.S. government agencies. As discussed earlier, the CIA must retain its own paramilitary capability. At the same time, the U.S. military must significantly increase its respective special operations capability to successfully conduct its counterterrorism and counterinsurgency missions.

Retired U.S. Army Special Forces Colonel Hy Rothstein addresses the need for the creation of a Directorate of Special Services (DSS), in his book *Afghanistan and the Troubled Future of Unconventional Warfare.* This organization would be staffed by officers from the various armed forces branches and select civilian agencies, and it would staff, train, and deploy to confront unconventional counterinsurgency and counterterrorist requirements. Rothstein clearly points out that the special operations community is underrepresented when policy decisions are being made in Washington, D.C. He suggests that the commander of the DSS have a seat on the Joint Chiefs of Staff (JCS). He also writes that the commander should be responsible for providing options, including placing unconventional forces in the lead in certain operations (which is almost never an option presently), to a president making a decision about the use of force.

In my view, the DSS should be formed by merging the U.S. armed forces' Special Operations Command (SOCOM) and the Intelligence and Security Command (INSCOM). This new organization should have the same authority to conduct covert action possessed by the CIA and be subject to the same degree of congressional oversight. Such a DSS would greatly enhance U.S. ability to deal with the broad need for unconventional skill sets. Though the CIA will likely reject the idea, its leadership must at the same time realize that the mere few hundred officers comprising the CIA's Special Activities Division cannot adequately deal with the two large unconventional conflicts the United States is currently engaged in. The DSS should aid in U.S. covert actions but should not replace the CIA as the principal FI collection agency in the U.S. government. During the Republican presidential primaries for the election in 2008, candidate John McCain spoke of the need to recreate an organization in the image of the World War II Office of Strategic Services (OSS) to conduct covert action missions. A DSS staffed by officers from the various branches of the armed forces and select civilian agencies would fit the bill.

CRITICAL POINT

- The special operations community is underrepresented when policy decisions are being made in Washington. The creation of a Directorate of Strategic Services would give the president a wider array of options and help him or her decide whether or not to use force.

17. THE PRESIDENT'S FOREIGN INTELLIGENCE ADVISORY BOARD

The President's Foreign Intelligence Advisory Board (PFIAB) provides advice to the president regarding the quality and effectiveness of intelligence collection, analysis and estimates, counterintelligence, and other intelligence activities. In 2008, the PFIAB consisted of sixteen members, all of whom were selected by the president. The PFIAB is tasked with providing the president with independent evaluation regarding the effectiveness of the intelligence community's ability to meet policymakers' needs in providing accurate and timely intelligence.

The PFIAB was first created by President Dwight D. Eisenhower in 1956 and was then called the President's Board of Consultants on Foreign Intelligence Activities. It was renamed during President John F. Kennedy's administration. Since its creation, the PFIAB has acted as a nonpartisan advisory board.

The PFIAB has had some distinguished and qualified chairmen such as former Senator Warren Rudman, former House Speaker Thomas Foley, former National Security Adviser Brent Scowcroft, and former Defense Secretary Les Aspin. Presidential selections to the PFIAB have been made in the belief that those from outside the government with a record of achievement, experience, independence, and integrity would bring with them special skills and knowledge that would enhance the intelligence community. Unfortunately, presidents have also used the PFIAB as a political reward to campaign contributors who were competent in various disciplines but actually did not contribute in a meaningful way to improving the intelligence community's performance. A president must resist placing individuals on the PFIAB to reward less than fully qualified individuals to whom political debts are owed. The importance of human intelligence collection in today's political climate makes it imperative that PFIAB members be plucked from areas of greatest benefit to achieving HUMINT capability.

In my review of recent lists of PFIAB membership, I found that no Islamic scholars had been members. Given current U.S. difficulties in the Middle East, someone with extensive knowledge of Islamic culture, like Professor Fouad Ajami from Johns Hopkins University, would be most helpful on the PFIAB. An expert on terrorism from academia would also be a beneficial addition to the board. Ken Alibek and others with similar experience in biological warfare would make an enormous contribution. Given the importance in this age of dealing with failed governments and efforts at nation building, former Department of State officers would be apt choices. At least one former member of the CIA's clandestine service, specifically a former deputy director of operations, should also be given a position on the PFIAB in order to bring to the board the necessary understanding of conflict and HUMINT. Someone like former ambassador and CIA case officer James Lilly would bring the secondary and critical experience of having dealt directly with China's leadership. An expert on missile technology and other potential military threats could be pulled from corporate America.

A secondary function of the PFIAB is to ensure that ongoing intelligence activities are in accordance with U.S. law and not contrary to executive order or presidential directive. The Intelligence Oversight Board (IOB) is a four-person standing committee within the PFIAB that serves this function. The person designated to lead the IOB should be a former CIA inspector general.

Much has been said and written about the intelligence failures that led to the attacks on September 11, 2001, and the failures associated with accurately assessing Iraq's weapons of mass destruction programs. The intended benefit of the PFIAB is to advise the president in a manner that allows him or her to preempt intelligence lapses. We do not need the PFIAB to serve as an investigative body after an event.

CRITICAL POINT

- The PFIAB must be staffed with individuals with the experience to provide added value to the intelligence community. Experts in Islamic culture, missile technology, postwar reconstruction, and redevelopment must be among its members.

18. NARCO-TERRORISM

In the 1970s and 1980s we witnessed the drug trade mature. Narco-traffickers in Southeast Asia and Latin America began penetrating the U.S. market with larger shipments of heroin and cocaine and thus gained the attention of policymakers. The Bureau of Narcotics and Dangerous Drugs (BNDD) conducted early national counternarcotics efforts. The BNDD became the Drug Enforcement Agency (DEA) in 1973.

COCAINE TRAFFICKING

A combination of factors, including an end to hostilities in Southeast Asia, withdrawal of a half million U.S. soldiers from the theater, and increased U.S. counternarcotic efforts against Southeast Asian heroin distribution, led to a reduction in the prevalence of heroin in the U.S. market, but cocaine, pushed across the borders by men like Carlos Lehder in the 1980s, soon became king. As America's illicit desire for cocaine grew, various Colombian criminal and insurgent groups increased production of the drug and built new distribution networks.

The Colombian government, under pressure from the United States, began to arrest and prosecute narco-traffickers to the full measure of the law. Narco-traffickers like Pablo Escobar responded to the government's efforts with significant violence, including car bombings and hundreds of assassinations of politicians, judges, and police. The United States and Colombia agreed to extradite Colombian narco-traffickers into U.S. prisons. Colombian narco-traffickers, fearful of the U.S. prison system because they could not negotiate release via U.S. law, resorted to kidnapping members of key political families in hopes of bringing the extradition policy to a halt. The term *narco-terrorism* was born out of the violence of this period in Colombia, violence that Colombia still suffers today.[1]

The Revolutionary Armed Forces of Colombia (Fuerzas Armadas Revolucionarias de Colombia), an armed group of between six and eight thousand fighters in southeastern Colombia, is considered a terrorist organization by the United States, Canada, and the European Union. The FARC controls between 15 and 20 percent of Colombian territory. The organization was born out of political violence and a right-wing military coup in the early 1950s and served as the military wing of the Communist Party of Colombia in the 1960s. In the 1980s it separated from the Communist Party and entered the narcotics trade, while still claiming to fight privatization of natural resources and entry of multinational corporations into Colombia. FARC leaders have made it clear in statements that they desire to seize power in the country. The FARC has a well-established record of murdering civilians, kidnapping noncombatants, and impressing underage fighters into its army. Escaped fighters, in multiple interviews, have admitted to their participation in and observation of sexual abuse and the exploitation of girls. The FARC has employed hostage-taking for both financial and political leverage and has even held prisoners for as long as decades and allowed hostages to die in captivity.

Cocaine trafficking drives the FARC organization's logistics and manpower. Unfortunately, the FARC is not the only narco-terrorist organization in Colombia. The National Liberation Army (Ejército de Liberación National) and the right-wing United Self-Defense Forces of Colombia (Autodefensas Unidas de Colombia) employ similar levels of violence in support of their narco-trafficking activities.

Mexican criminal organizations in the late 1990s used their proximity to the United States and links to Colombian narcotic producers to establish cocaine distribution networks. Groups like the Arellano-Felix drug cartel operating out of Tijuana used cocaine profits to co-opt the local police and the Mexican army in support of their illicit activities. Assassinations, kidnapping, and torture became part of the business plan, putting these groups in the narco-terrorist category. The equivalent of an entire Mexican army unit,

---

[1] Mark Bowden, *Killing Pablo: The Hunt for the World's Greatest Outlaw* (New York: Penguin Books, 2001).

after receiving special operations training from various military forces from around the world, defected to the narco-traffickers. The group, known as the Zetas (Los Zetas), shoots, moves, and communicates on behalf of Mexican narco-interests along the U.S.-Mexican border. During the last few years, the Zetas have been implicated in assassinations on the U.S. side of the border.

THE TALIBAN AND OPIUM

The Taliban, originally a Pakistani supported Islamic force led by the charismatic Mullah Omar, replaced warring mujahideen groups in Afghanistan in the mid-1990s.[2] The Taliban initially reduced production of opium, the principal component of heroin, in Afghanistan, but later in its reign selectively increased production to augment its coffers, given its political and economic isolation. Currently the Taliban operates from Pakistan's Northwest Frontier Province and federally administered tribal areas (FATA), and opium production funds the violence the group exacts against the Afghan people, the Islamic Republic of Afghanistan (IROA), and U.S. coalition forces still in the country. The Taliban and its anti-coalition militant (ACM) forces have conducted thousands of IED, human bomb, and vehicular attacks on civilians and coalition forces in Afghanistan. The Taliban has destroyed over a thousand schools and clinics and continues to oppose the education of girls. While the Taliban, unlike the FARC, is not motivated to deal in narcotics simply for profit, opium is the engine driving its violent machine.

Though the United States has led significant efforts against narco-terrorism in the Western Hemisphere, it hasn't yet made much of an effort in Afghanistan. Ninety-seven percent of the world's opium comes from Afghanistan. Fifty percent of Afghanistan's opium comes from Helmand Province in southern Afghanistan. Helmand Province is home to only 5.6 percent of Afghanistan's population.[3] Thus, the U.S. government should seriously consider conducting eradication as a strategy in Helmand. Angering Helmand's tiny population in order to destroy the mother load of

---

[2] Ahmad Rashid, *Taliban: Militant Islam Oil and Fundamentalism in Central Asia* (New Haven: Yale University Press, 2001).

[3] Thomas Schweich (comp.), *U.S. Counternarcotics Strategy for Afghanistan, 2007* (Washington, DC: U.S. Department of State, August 2007).

the Taliban's opium production and funding would be a worthwhile endeavor. Yet, the Afghan government has rejected aerial spraying as a technique for eradication to date. The Afghan poppy fields are large enough that someone standing on the moon looking back at earth with a standard three-foot telescope could see them. To assume eradication forces can manually destroy such huge poppy fields with tractors is absurd. In addition, manual eradication techniques are easily targeted by narco-traffickers, who can booby-trap fields with mines and IEDs. Explosives bring the eradication process to a standstill until the area can be secured and cleared by EOD personnel. Aerial spraying, with forces positioned around target areas to protect aircraft, is far more practical: spraying can cover more ground more quickly and the additional forces will cut down on or eliminate Taliban interference.

When considering the situation in Aghanistan, it is important to understand that many elected officials and members of the Afghan security forces profit from the opium trade. If pressured to spray, they will cry that Afghanistan's sovereignty is being violated, but truthfully their major concern is maintaining their own profits from the illicit opium trade. A dual track of eradication and interdiction must be employed against the Afghan opium problem. Only when opium production and trafficking is suppressed will we make significant headway against the Taliban.

CRITICAL POINTS

- Terrorist groups, like other enterprises, need financial resources. Narco-trafficking provides the large and steady cash flow necessary to support the groups' other goals.

- Future presidents should continue U.S. support of the Colombian government in its fight against narco-terrorists such as the FARC and ELN.

- Colombian groups and the Taliban are dependent on profits from the narcotics trade and are vulnerable if those profits can be sufficiently reduced.

- The next president must pressure the Afghan government to conduct aerial spraying as part of counternarcotics strategy in Afghanistan.

19. CONCLUSIONS

It became clear in 2008 that the additional surge of U.S. forces in Iraq had produced positive results. The alliance of Sunni tribes of Iraq's western Anbar Province with U.S. forces, referred to as "the awakening," resulted in combat success against al Qaeda elements in Anbar Province and improved the security situation for the population at large.

Significant violence continues in Iraq, although it has been diminished from what can only be described as horrific levels. This violence is a result of a persistent al Qaeda presence, sectarian violence supported by Iran, and lethal entrepreneurial activities by the tens of thousands of unemployed and underemployed Iraqis who are not jihadists or supporters of Islamic rule but who participate in kidnappings or the planting of IEDs solely to make a living.

George W. Bush's administration lacked a plan for the post-invasion period in Iraq. It failed to deploy sufficient troops to maintain order and secure Iraq's gigantic stockpiles of weaponry and explosives. This administration also displayed a stubborn unwillingness to heed calls by U.S. intelligence officers in the field, who reported that an insurgency was under way early on. These combined failures contributed greatly to the intensity and duration of the violence in Iraq. A Pew poll taken in Iraq in 2008 estimated that over one million Iraqis had died since 2003.

Those who frame this violence simply in terms of "the war on terrorism" fail to comprehend the hostility felt by a sizable segment of the population of Iraq and others in the Middle East who condemn our presence as an occupation. The United States is partly culpable for the loss of control in Iraq. As former secretary of state Colin Powell said to President Bush, Vice President Cheney, and Secretary of Defense Donald Rumsfeld in regard to Iraq, "You break it, you own it." Equally important is understanding that the growing chorus of calls to set an immediate and complete withdrawal of U.S. forces opens the possibility for an even larger human catastrophe.

The incoming president will have to focus efforts on maintaining security and stability and building a political consensus among Iraq's various ethnic and religious communities. Withdrawal simply for the sake of washing our hands of Iraq is likely to unleash at least another wave of significant violence. Such a wave may not reach our shores but risks enveloping our regional allies, crushing them, and dragging them into the sea. Campaign promises based on a theme of withdrawal, withdrawal, withdrawal—even when preceded by the word "responsible"—provide comfort to our enemies. The next president must devote time to finding a way to improve the situation on the ground in order to improve both the security situation and the lives of Iraqis fighting so desperately for a better life for themselves and their families.

The issue of governance in Iraq must be addressed within the larger context of national reconciliation and apportionment of the wealth derived by Iraq's oil. It is likely that over time and with the changes in demographics resulting from ethnic violence, Iraq's three primary constituent parts will move toward a federal system highly independent of one another.

The creation of a stabilization force, initially half the size of the existing force of 150,000 in Iraq, might be sufficient to combat a resurgence of al Qaeda and maintain security. Over time, this force could be reduced in number. Such a force would be a significant commitment and would allow for a maneuver force with ground and air assets that could quickly influence events on the ground. With continued advancement, U.S. and coalition forces could transition to such a role in two or three years. Such a force would also restore U.S. military power vis-à-vis Iran, our main regional adversary.

I understand the frustration of those who want an immediate and complete withdrawal from Iraq. I do not question their patriotism. I too am heartbroken by the number of dead and wounded servicemen and women. Both of my children are in the armed forces. I pray for their safety every day. Unfortunately, an Iraqi government unable to call on a nearby emergency force for security support in times of crisis is likely to fail. There will be no perfect plan for Iraq, but we must seek a plan that allows us to maximize our influence while minimizing our exposure and the possibility that violence will spiral out of control. I am not suggesting writing the Iraqi political leadership a blank check. All the instruments of American power need to be brought to bear to ensure Iraqi national reconciliation.

As for the forgotten war—Afghanistan—the United States needs to augment the current deployment of combat force—two airborne brigade combat teams of 3,500 soldiers each in the east and a Marine expeditionary unit in the south—with at least one more airborne brigade and accompanying air assets. Additionally, the Freedom Corps, as described in chapter 8, needs to be created and deployed in Afghanistan as a response to and recognition that this is going to be a long-term problem requiring out-of-the-box thinking. It is imperative that the United States and its coalition partners accomplish the mission in Afghanistan. As stated in chapter 9, the successful launching and funding of a robust Afghan-U.S. integrated intelligence and counterinsurgency effort would yield positive results and further enhance the defense of Afghanistan.

I do not believe that presidents should delegate all but their most significant decisions and seek to be completely above the fray. We live in a complex world. As of 2008, we are at war in two countries. An incoming president needs to role up his or her sleeves and dive in to fix the problems that most threaten the safety and welfare of the citizens of our country and the soldiers and civilians who defend us. When it comes to intelligence and counterterrorism, presidential competence counts. Though it might be politically convenient for a president to distance him or herself from the intelligence and counterterrorism community in order to claim ignorance of organizational difficulties and shortfalls in performance, this does not serve the interests of the nation. What happens in the intelligence and counterterrorism community matters to all Americans. Because much that goes on in that arena is done out of the public eye, we rely on the president to ensure that those activities are conducted competently and in accordance with U.S. law. More often than not, those elected president have not been up to the task. It is my hope that this book will help an incoming president and staff prepare for the challenges ahead while simultaneously informing the public so that they will be better prepared to hold their leaders accountable.

GLOSSARY

Air India Flight 814 (IC-814): Five Pakistani Kashmiri men hijacked this flight on December 24, 1999, shortly after takeoff from Kathmandu's Tribhuvan International Airport. The flight was en route to Indira Gandhi International Airport in New Dehli, India. The hijackers initially directed the plane to land in Lahore, Pakistan, but when they were denied landing there, they stopped to refuel in Amritsar, India. In Amritsar the hijackers stabbed and killed one man. After several more refueling stops, the plane landed in Kandahar, Afghanistan, and Indian officials began negotiations with the hijackers. The passengers were released on December 31 in exchange for the release of three Muslim extremists held in India.

Allende, Salvador (1908–1973): President of Chile from 1970 to 1973 who established diplomatic relations with Cuba and closer relations with other communist countries. Allende nationalized industries that had U.S. business interests, which cost him the support of Chile's business sector. In September 1973 the army attacked the presidential palace and found him dead by a self-inflicted gunshot wound.

Al Qaeda: An international alliance of Sunni militants founded in the late 1980s by Saudi citizen Osama bin Laden and his Egyptian deputy, **Dr. Ayman al-Zawahiri**. Al Qaeda, meaning "the base" in Arabic, executed the September 11, 2001, attacks on the United States. In addition to attacking Western interests, al Qaeda has committed itself to driving coalition forces from Iraq and Afghanistan through attacks on local forces, the coalition forces, and the host nation's civilian population.

Ames, Aldrich (1941–): Thirty-one-year veteran of the CIA who pled guilty to spying for the Russians. In 1994 Ames was sentenced to life in prison without the possibility of parole.

Associate deputy director of operations: This title, currently not in use, refers to the second in command of the CIA's Clandestine Service.

Autodefensas Unidas de Colombia (AUC): The United Self-Defense Forces of Colombia is an umbrella organization of right-wing paramilitary organizations that operated primarily in northern Colombia. The organization works in coordination with Colombian drug cartels and fought leftist guerrillas of the **Fuerzas Armadas Revolucionarias de Colombia (FARC)**. In 2006 Colombian president Alvaro Uribe negotiated the demobilization of the AUC. Over thirty thousand AUC members laid down their weapons. In 2008 AUC leader Carlos Mario Jimenez was extradited to the United States for his continued involvement in narcotics trafficking from inside a Colombian prison.

Aum Shinrikyo: The Japanese religious cult founded by the charismatic blind figure Shoko Asahara in 1984. Asahara incorporated a combination of Buddhist and Hindu tenets into the cult's belief system. The group was given the nickname "Doomsday Cult" based on Asahara's desire to cause a global conflict that would allow for his ascension to world power via the use of WMDs against modern nation-states. Aum conducted the 1995 Tokyo sarin attacks. The group was reported to have undertaken significant recruitment efforts, and its membership in Moscow reached ten thousand in the early 1990s. Aum Shinrikyo has renamed itself Aleph. It currently has fifteen hundred members, three hundred of which are in Russia.

Beslan school hostage crisis: On September 1, 2004, Chechen terrorists took hundreds of students and adults hostage at Beslan's Secondary School Number One in North Ossetia-Alania, Russia. On September 3, 2004, an explosion, likely a mishap caused by one of the terrorists, initiated an escalating exchange of gunfire and then all-out assault on the school by security forces and the population. In the chaos, 334 perished, including 186 of the children hostages.

Bhopal disaster: The world's worst industrial accident occurred in Bhopal, India, on December 3, 1984, when forty tons of methyl isocyanate (MIC) gas were released into the atmosphere at Bhopal's

Union Carbide subsidiary pesticide plant. Close to 500,000 people were exposed to the leaking gas, and 3,800 died immediately. It is estimated that twenty thousand have died prematurely over the years as a result of injuries incurred in the disaster.

Bureau of Diplomatic Security: Security and law enforcement element within the U.S. Department of State that manages the physical security of U.S. diplomatic missions and personnel abroad and participates in international investigations on the issues of cybersecurity, counterterrorism, and various other crimes that have an impact on U.S. interests.

Castro, Fidel (1926–): Revolutionary leader who seized power from Cuban dictator Fulgencio Batista in 1959. Castro was the first secretary of the Communist Party of Cuba and dictator of Cuba until 2008, when because of age and ill health he turned power over to his younger brother, Raul Castro. During much of the 1960s, 1970s, and 1980s, Castro's Cuba was a prime surrogate of the Soviet Union and participated in and supported the deployment of Cuban forces in covert and overt wars in Latin America and Africa. In 2007 *Forbes* magazine included Fidel Castro on its list of the world's richest men. Castro complained bitterly about his inclusion on this list.

Chávez, Hugo (1954–): Venezuelan military officer who led a failed military coup in 1992 and who in 1998 was elected president of Venezuela. Chávez, a vehement critic of the United States, has used Venezuelan oil wealth as a means to support populist policies at home and fund and organize his Revolutionary Bolivarian Movement abroad. Following the Soviet Union's collapse, Chávez's Venezuela has assumed the financing of Cuba's continued communist experiment. This has included the provision of large subsidies of petroleum and continued political and financial support to Cuban interventionist activities in other Latin American countries.

Chief of station (COS): CIA's senior officer on the ground in a foreign country. Almost always a member of the Clandestine Service, the COS is the DCIA's personal representative in the country where he or she is assigned. The COS also serves as the principal adviser on intelligence issues to the U.S. ambassador assigned in his or her country. The COS manages operations officers in the acquisition and handling of human sources, including officials within hostile governments and terrorist organizations, weapons proliferators, and narco-traffickers threatening U.S. interests.

Covert action: Any action employed by a government or entity to achieve some political or military result in which the initiating party conceals its involvement, support, or initiation of the act. In the United States, the CIA is the principal arm of the U.S. government that conducts covert action. A signed presidential finding is required to proceed with such actions. The **Department of Defense** is authorized to conduct covert action in support of armed conflict.

Department of Defense (DOD): Federal department responsible for supervising and coordinating the various branches of the U.S. armed forces. The DOD comprises the Department of the Army, Department of the Navy, Department of the Air Force, and more than a dozen other defense-related agencies.

Department of State (DOS): Federal department that manages U.S. foreign affairs. The Department of State is led by the secretary of state, who is appointed by the president and confirmed by the U.S. Senate. The U.S. Foreign Service, which staffs U.S. diplomatic missions abroad, is a critical component of the Department of State.

Deputy chief of mission (DCM): Second most senior member of a U.S. foreign diplomatic mission (or embassy) after an ambassador. DCMs are almost always career foreign service officers and handle the day-to-day management of U.S. embassies.

Defense Intelligence Agency (DIA): Significant producer and manager of military intelligence under DOD. Its principal role is to provide military intelligence to the regional combatant commanders and defense policymakers. The DIA was created in 1961.

Drug Enforcement Agency (DEA): Section of the U.S. Department of Justice tasked with fighting the illegal production and distribution of narcotics. DEA agents investigate and combat criminal narcotic organizations at home and abroad. The DEA was established on July 1, 1973, and succeeded the disbanded Bureau of Narcotics and Dangerous Drugs.

East Africa Bombings: On August 7, 1998, near simultaneous car-bomb attacks on the U.S. embassies in Dar es Salaam, Tanzania, and Nairobi, Kenya, were directed by al Qaeda leader Osama bin Laden. The attacks resulted in the deaths of over 270 people and the injury of a thousand local nationals. As a result of these attacks bin Laden was placed on the FBI's ten most wanted list.

Escobar, Pablo (1949–1993): Noted Colombian Medellín drug cartel leader. Escobar was one of the most violent and ambitious narco-traffickers in history. He was responsible for the death and kidnapping of dozens of Colombian judges and other officials and family members as well as the murder of hundreds of Colombian police officers.

Espionage: Craft of managing human sources and spies in the midst of competitors and adversaries. Sun Tzu's classic work, *The Art of War*, written approximately two thousand years ago is still a relevant treatise on the importance of espionage in conflict.

Extradition: Process by which one government makes an official request to a second government to facilitate the surrender and transport of a suspect to the territory of the first government to allow for prosecution.

Fuerzas Armadas Revolucionarias de Colombia (FARC): Organization that grew from the military wing of Colombia's Communist Party in the 1960s, which initiates guerrilla and revolutionary activities, including narco-trafficking. The FARC currently fields between six and eight thousand fighters and operates in and controls large segments of Colombia's southeastern jungles. It is considered a terrorist group by the United States and the European Union.

Foreign intelligence (FI): CIA's primary responsibility, providing intelligence on the plans and intentions of foreign adversaries or competitors. This includes political, economic, military, and scientific information. FI reporting is designed to support U.S. policymaking.

Hamas (Harakat al-Muqawama al-Islamiyya): Islamic Resistance Movement, a Palestinian Sunni Islamic political and terrorist organization created in 1987 by Sheikh Ahmad Yasin, a member of the Muslim Brotherhood. Hamas advocates the destruction of the State of Israel and is known for having conducted hundreds of suicide bombings against both Israeli military and civilian targets. Since

2006 it has taken control of the administration in the Gaza Strip. It is considered a terrorist organization by the United States.

Hanssen, Robert (1944–): FBI agent who spied for the Russians for more than twenty years. His activities have been called "possibly the worst intelligence disaster in U.S. history." He is serving a life sentence in solitary confinement.

Hawala: Unregulated informal value transfer system for moving funds resembling an illegal Western Union made up of independent brokers primarily based in Asia, Africa, and the Middle East.

Hezbollah: Party of God, a Lebanese Shiite political movement that has political, social, and terrorist components. Hezbollah's spiritual leader is Sheikh Mohammed Hussein Fadlallah, and its secretary general is Hassan Nasrallah. Hezbollah was formed after the Israeli military invasion of Lebanon in 1982. With the support of Iran, Lebanese Shia developed cells to fight the Israeli occupation and conducted attacks on U.S. and other Western interests. Hezbollah has conducted numerous high-profile terrorist attacks against Israel, the United States, and other Western powers around the globe.

Humala, Ollanta: Peruvian leftist candidate for president in 2006 who was defeated by Alan García. As a Peruvian army officer Humala led an unsuccessful military coup in 2000. He was pardoned for the action after Peruvian president Alberto Fujimori fled Peru and was impeached.

Human intelligence (HUMINT): The means by which intelligence is collected from human sources, be they clandestine sources or prisoners under interrogation.

Improvised explosive device (IED): Bomb constructed and deployed in ways other than in conventional military action. IEDs may be fabricated with either military explosives or industrial chemical compounds designed to kill civilians or military personnel. Frequently they are concealed underground, in a vehicle, or on a person's body to allow the attacker proximity to a target. IEDs are the new weapon of choice in asymmetrical warfare.

Iran hostage crisis: On November 4, 1979, radical Iranian students seized the U.S. embassy in Tehran, Iran. For 444 days, fifty-two American diplomats and military personnel assigned to the U.S. embassy were held as hostages in violation of international conventions and laws. A failed rescue effort on April 24, 1980, resulted in the death of eight U.S. military personnel. The hostages were released moments before Ronald Reagan was sworn in as president of the United States.

Jihad: Islamic term to describe the religious duty of Muslims to strive or struggle in the way of God. A person engaged in jihad is called a mujahid; the plural of the term is mujahideen. The term *jihad* has come to be most closely associated with the struggle of Muslims fighting against non-Muslims in a holy or religious war.

Khan, Abdul Qadir (1936–): Scientist known as the father of Pakistan's nuclear weapons program. A. Q. Khan was at the heart of an international network proliferating nuclear technology to Libya, Iran, and North Korea. Under U.S. pressure, he confessed his involvement in the network on February 4, 2004, on Pakistani television and was then held under house arrest. Khan was subsequently pardoned by Pakistani president Pervez Musharraf.

Kuwait Airways Flight 422: Flight hijacked while en route from Bangkok to Kuwait on April 5, 1988. The hijacking was a fifteen-day crisis during which the aircraft landed in Iran, Cyprus, and finally Algeria. While in Iran, the Iranian Islamic Republic allowed additional Hezbollah terrorists to join those who had seized the plane and also allowed the terrorists to be provided with additional weapons. The hijackers murdered two Kuwaiti citizens. In Algeria the terrorists freed their hostages and were permitted to fly to freedom in either Lebanon or Iran.

Legal attaché: FBI officers assigned under diplomatic status abroad to a U.S. embassy.

Lehder, Carlos (1950–): Leader of the transportation/smuggling component of the Medellín cartel. In the 1970s Lehder used small aircraft from the Bahamian island of Norman's Cay to establish a significant criminal enterprise. He was eventually forced to flee the Bahamas and return to Colombia, where he was captured in the jungle and then extradited to the United States. His wealth was estimated at more than 2 billion dollars. He is currently serving an extended prison sentence in the United States.

Liberation Tigers of Tamil Eelam (LTTE): Tamil militant group in northern Sri Lanka led by Velupillai Pirapaharan. Founded by Pirapaharan in the 1970s, the group made its first significant attacks in the early 1980s. The LTTE has fought to carve out a Tamil state in Sri Lanka's Tamil-dominated northern Jaffna peninsula and multiethnic eastern provinces. The Tigers are famous for wearing cyanide capsules on strings around their necks so that they can commit suicide before being captured. India first secretly funded and supported the LTTE and then subsequently invaded northern Sri Lanka with eighty thousand soldiers to assist the Sri Lankan security forces in an effort to suppress the LTTE. The LTTE revolutionized suicide terrorist attacks and has used bicycles, motorcycles, buses, and boats to deliver **improvised explosive devices** against targets.

McVeigh, Timothy: Perpetrator of the April 19, 1995, Oklahoma City Bombing, during which 168 people died and more than 800 were injured. This was the single largest act of domestic terrorism in U.S. history. McVeigh built an IED consisting of ammonium nitrate and high-octane fuel and transported the device to the front of Oklahoma City's Alfred P. Murrah Federal Building for detonation. He was taken into custody when police stopped him for driving a vehicle without a license plate. Shortly after his arrest, he was identified as a suspect in the attack. McVeigh was motivated by anger at the U.S. federal response to events at the Branch Davidian cult in Waco, Texas, in 1993 and in Ruby Ridge, Idaho, in 1992, which he claimed were excesses by the FBI. McVeigh was executed on June 11, 2001.

Morales, Evo (1959–): President of Bolivia and leader of the Bolivian Cocalero Movement (Federation of Coca Growers), which resists eradication efforts in Bolivia's Chapare Province. Morales employed the cocaleros, other leftists, Colombian terrorist mentorship, and Venezuelan cash in a campaign of violence against several Bolivian presidents to destabilize the country and ultimately pave the way for his election.

Nicholson, Harold J. (1950–): Former CIA officer arrested in 1996 for espionage. He pled guilty to spying for Russia, including supplying that country with biographical information for every CIA case officer trained during 1994–1996, and was sentenced to twenty-three years in prison.

Operations officer: CIA officer, historically known as a case officer, whose responsibilities include the recruitment and management of clandestine sources. Operations officers serve the majority of their careers in the CIA's Clandestine Service. They are hired and trained under the CIA's Career Service Trainee (CST) program.

Radio Farda (Radio Tomorrow): Persian/Farsi radio station funded by the U.S. government. Farda broadcasts news, political commentary, and cultural stories directed toward the Iranian population. The station is funded using the model established for Radio Free Europe during the Cold War.

Rendition: Lawful handing over of a suspect or criminal when a legal process of extradition does not exist between two governments.

Zarqawi, Abu Musab al- (1966–2006): Jordanian Sunni terrorist who ran terrorist training camps in Afghanistan. Zarqawi relocated to northern Iraq after the fall of the Taliban and created Jamaat al-Tawhid wa'l-Jihad, which later became al Qaeda in Iraq. Zarqawi conducted significant attacks on coalition forces and Shia religious targets in an effort to foment a Sunni-Shia civil war. He was killed by U.S. forces on June 7, 2006.

Zawahiri, Ayman al- (1951–): Second in command of al Qaeda and leader of Egyptian Islamic Jihad. A surgeon by trade, Zawahiri was arrested following the assassination of Egyptian president Anwar Sadat on October 6, 1981 and tortured during his incarceration in Egypt. He fled Egypt on his release and joined Palestinian Islamic leader Sheikh Abdullah Yusuf Azzam in Afghanistan during the early days of the Afghan Soviet Jihad. During this time Zawahiri and Osama bin Laden began their association and joint efforts.

CHRONOLOGY OF CIA DIRECTORS

TRUMAN

1946	R.Adm. Sidney William Souers, U.S. Naval Reserve	
1946–1947	Lt. Gen. Hoyt Sanford Vandenberg, Army Air Forces	
1947–1950	R.Adm. Roscoe Henry Hillenkoetter, U.S. Navy	
1950–1953	Gen. Walter Bedell Smith, U.S. Army	
1953–1961	Allen Welsh Dulles	EISENHOWER
1961–1965	John Alex McCone	KENNEDY
1965–1966	V.Adm. William Francis Raborn Jr., U.S. Navy	JOHNSON
1966–1973	Richard McGarrah Helms	JOHNSON
1973	James Rodney Schlesinger	NIXON
1973–1976	William Egan Colby	NIXON
1976–1977	George Herbert Walker Bush	FORD
1977–1981	Adm. Stansfield Turner, U.S. Navy	CARTER
1981–1987	William Joseph Casey	REAGAN
1987–1991	William Hedgcock Webster	REAGAN
1991–1993	Robert Michael Gates	BUSH I
1993–1995	Robert James Woolsey Jr.	CLINTON
1995–1997	John Mark Deutch	CLINTON
1997–2004	George John Tenet	CLINTON
2004–2006	Porter Johnston Goss	BUSH II
2006–present	Gen. Michael Vincent Hayden, U.S. Air Force	BUSH II

_20 y_

_40 y_

_50 y_

2009

2004–2013 Leon E. Panetta

2013 – ?

RECOMMENDED READING

Alibek, Ken, and Stephen Handelman. *Biohazard: The Chilling True Story of the Largest Covert Biological Weapons Program in the World—Told from the Inside by the Man Who Ran It.* New York: Random House, 1999.

This memoir discloses how an elite team of Russian bioweaponeers created and manufactured weapons of mass destruction during the Cold War era. Alibek revisits his dangerous time as a scientist in the bioweapons lab and discusses arms proliferation and terrorism.

Galula, David. *Counterinsurgency Warfare: Theory and Practice.* Westport, CT: Praeger Security International, 2006.

Originally written in 1964, this eerily relevant book by a former French military officer analyzes how to fight insurgency efficiently and the deterrents that may arise during such an effort.

Hoffman, Bruce. *Inside Terrorism.* Rev. and exp. ed. New York: Columbia University Press, 2006.

Inside Terrorism charts the major historical movements of international terrorism. It also provides insight into the impetus behind political and religious terrorism and why a greater amount of violence can be expected in the future.

Hussain, Zahid. *Frontline Pakistan: The Struggle with Militant Islam.* New York: Columbia University Press, 2007.

Here Hussain reveals the growing activity of Islamic extremists in Pakistan and carefully addresses the connections between Inter-Services Intelligence (ISI), a governmental branch; al Qaeda; and the major jihadi groups located in the country.

Nagl, John A. *Counterinsurgency Lessons from Malaya and Vietnam: Learning to Eat Soup with a Knife.* Westport, CT: Praeger Publishers, 2002, hardcover edition; published in paperback as *Learning to Eat Soup with a Knife: Counterinsurgency Lessons from Malaya and Vietnam.* Chicago: University of Chicago Press, 2005.

Lieutenant Colonel Nagl uses the comparison of the counterinsurgency doctrine developed during the Malayan Emergency (1948–1960) with that developed during the Vietnam War (1950–1975) to address the overarching issue of how armies that are originally unprepared for a conflict adjust to their changing environment.

Nasr, Vali. *The Shia Revival: How Conflicts within Islam Will Shape the Future.* New York: Norton, 2006.

This book outlines the history and theology of Shia Islam and details its strained relationship with the dominant Sunni faith. Nasr argues that with the instability in the Middle East the Shia Crescent is becoming more and more powerful and that this repositioning could have dramatic ramifications.

Phillips, Donald T. *Lincoln on Leadership: Executive Strategies for Tough Times.* New York: Warner Books, 1992.

Phillips analyzes Abraham Lincoln's unusual leadership techniques and proposes how they can be effectively utilized in present-day society.

Pillar, Paul R. *Terrorism and U.S. Foreign Policy.* Washington, DC: Brookings Institution Press, 2001.

In this book, Pillar examines various aspects of terrorism and counterterrorism and suggests ways to improve U.S. counterterrorism policy. He reasons that increased coordination between conventional foreign policy and counterterrorism efforts would be the most effective approach to preventing terrorist attacks.

Rosen, Nir. *In the Belly of the Green Bird: The Triumph of the Martyrs in Iraq.* New York: Free Press, 2006, hardcover edition; published in paperback as *Triumph of the Martyrs: A Reporter's Journey into Occupied Iraq.* Washington, DC: Potomac Books, 2008.

As a freelance journalist in Iraq from 2003 to 2005, Rosen gained access to many diverse areas of Iraqi society, from Shia and Sunni resistance groups to ordinary Iraqi civilians, and from his experiences he penned a comprehensive account of Iraq's sectarian conflict.

Rothstein, Hy S. *Afghanistan and the Troubled Future of Unconventional Warfare.* Annapolis, MD: Naval Institute Press, 2006.

Here, Rothstein uses the U.S. war with Afghanistan as a case study to examine the "conventionalization" of American warfare in spite of continuous efforts to strengthen the unconventional warfare tactics used by U.S. troops in the Middle East. Rothstein offers ideas about how the United States could gain these essential warfare abilities, for he views a strong unconventional warfare program as key to a decisive U.S. victory in the Middle East.

Scheuer, Michael. *Through Our Enemies' Eyes: Osama Bin Laden, Radical Islam, and the Future of America.* Rev. ed. Washington, DC: Potomac Books, 2006.

This book explores the U.S. view of itself and its enemy in the Middle East. Scheuer explains how Western society and culture are the primary reasons radical Muslims have declared war on the Western world. He suggests that understanding the enemy's view of itself and the United States, and adjusting Western rhetoric accordingly, is the only way to decrease the threat to U.S. national security posed by radical Muslims.

INDEX

ABOUT THE AUTHOR

Gary Berntsen is a retired senior CIA operations officer who has served as a chief of station on three separate occasions. He led the CIA's most important counterterrorist deployments from 1995 through 2005. Since May 2007 he has been serving as an intelligence and counterinsurgency adviser in eastern Afghanistan. Berntsen is the author of the bestseller *Jawbreaker: The Attack on Bin Laden and Al Qaeda* (Crown, 2005). He has made more than seventy-five television appearances, including numerous appearances on CNN, Fox, MSNBC, and NBC. He lives in Forest Hills, New York.